THE SACRAMENT OF CHARITY

SACRAMENTUM CARITATIS

POST-SYNODAL APOSTOLIC EXHORTATION

BENEDICT XVI

POST-SYNODAL
APOSTOLIC EXHORTATION
SACRAMENTUM CARITATIS
OF THE HOLY FATHER
BENEDICT XVI
TO THE BISHOPS, CLERGY,
CONSECRATED PERSONS
AND THE LAY FAITHFUL
ON THE EUCHARIST
AS THE SOURCE AND SUMMIT
OF THE CHURCH'S LIFE AND MISSION

Publication No. 7-002
United States Conference of Catholic Bishops
Washington, D.C.
ISBN 978-1-60137-002-0

© 2007 Libreria Editrice Vaticana
Vatican City

Published in the United States, March 2007

CONTENTS

INTRODUCTION

1. The sacrament of charity,[1] the Holy Eucharist is the gift that Jesus Christ makes of himself, thus revealing to us God's infinite love for every man and woman. This wondrous sacrament makes manifest that "greater" love which led him to "lay down his life for his friends" (Jn 15:13). Jesus did indeed love them "to the end" (Jn 13:1). In those words the Evangelist introduces Christ's act of immense humility: before dying for us on the Cross, he tied a towel around himself and washed the feet of his disciples. In the same way, Jesus continues, in the sacrament of the Eucharist, to love us "to the end," even to offering us his body and his blood. What amazement must the Apostles have felt in witnessing what the Lord did and said during that Supper! What wonder must the eucharistic mystery also awaken in our own hearts!

The food of truth

2. In the sacrament of the altar, the Lord meets us, men and women created in God's image and likeness (cf. Gen 1:27), and becomes our companion along the way. In this sacrament, the Lord truly becomes food for us, to satisfy our hunger for truth and freedom. Since only the truth can make us free (cf. Jn 8:32), Christ becomes for us the food of truth. With deep human insight, Saint Augustine clearly showed how we are moved spontaneously, and not by constraint, whenever we encounter something attractive and desirable. Asking himself what it is that can move us most deeply, the saintly Bishop went on to say: "What does our soul desire more passionately than truth?"[2] Each of us has an innate and irrepressible desire for ultimate and definitive truth. The Lord Jesus, "the way, and the truth, and the life" (Jn 14:6), speaks to our thirsting, pilgrim hearts, our hearts yearning for the source of life, our hearts longing for truth. Jesus Christ is the Truth in person, drawing the world to himself. "Jesus is the lodestar of human freedom: without him, freedom loses its focus, for without the knowledge of truth, freedom

1

becomes debased, alienated and reduced to empty caprice. With him, freedom finds itself."[3] In the sacrament of the Eucharist, Jesus shows us in particular the *truth about the love* which is the very essence of God. It is this evangelical truth which challenges each of us and our whole being. For this reason, the Church, which finds in the Eucharist the very center of her life, is constantly concerned to proclaim to all, *opportune importune* (cf. *2 Tim* 4:2), that God is love.[4] Precisely because Christ has become for us the food of truth, the Church turns to every man and woman, inviting them freely to accept God's gift.

The development of the eucharistic rite
3. If we consider the bimillenary history of God's Church, guided by the wisdom of the Holy Spirit, we can gratefully admire the orderly development of the ritual forms in which we commemorate the event of our salvation. From the varied forms of the early centuries, still resplendent in the rites of the Ancient Churches of the East, up to the spread of the Roman rite; from the clear indications of the Council of Trent and the Missal of Saint Pius V to the liturgical renewal called for by the Second Vatican Council: in every age of the Church's history the eucharistic celebration, as the source and summit of her life and mission, shines forth in the liturgical rite in all its richness and variety. The Eleventh Ordinary General Assembly of the Synod of Bishops, held from 2-23 October 2005 in the Vatican, gratefully acknowledged the guidance of the Holy Spirit in this rich history. In a particular way, the Synod Fathers acknowledged and reaffirmed the beneficial influence on the Church's life of the liturgical renewal which began with the Second Vatican Ecumenical Council.[5] The Synod of Bishops was able to evaluate the reception of the renewal in the years following the Council. There were many expressions of appreciation. The difficulties and even the occasional abuses which were noted, it was affirmed, cannot overshadow the benefits and the validity of the liturgical renewal, whose riches are yet to be fully explored. Concretely, the changes which the Council called for need to be understood within the overall unity of the historical development of the rite itself, without the introduction of artificial discontinuities.[6]

The Synod of Bishops and the Year of the Eucharist

4. We should also emphasize the relationship between the recent Synod of Bishops on the Eucharist and the events which have taken place in the Church's life in recent years. First of all, we should recall the Great Jubilee of the Year 2000, with which my beloved Predecessor, the Servant of God John Paul II, led the Church into the third Christian millennium. The Jubilee Year clearly had a significant eucharistic dimension. Nor can we forget that the Synod of Bishops was preceded, and in some sense prepared for, by the Year of the Eucharist which John Paul II had, with great foresight, wanted the whole Church to celebrate. That year, which began with the International Eucharistic Congress in Guadalajara in October 2004, ended on 23 October 2005, at the conclusion of the XI Synodal Assembly, with the canonization of five saints particularly distinguished for their eucharistic piety: Bishop Józef Bilczewski, Fathers Gaetano Catanoso, Zygmunt Gorazdowski and Alberto Hurtado Cruchaga, and the Capuchin Fra Felice da Nicosia. Thanks to the teachings proposed by John Paul II in the Apostolic Letter *Mane Nobiscum Domine*[7] and to the helpful suggestions of the Congregation for Divine Worship and the Discipline of the Sacraments,[8] many initiatives were undertaken by Dioceses and various ecclesial groups in order to reawaken and increase eucharistic faith, to improve the quality of eucharistic celebration, to promote eucharistic adoration and to encourage a practical solidarity which, starting from the Eucharist, would reach out to those in need. Finally, mention should be made of the significance of my venerable Predecessor's last Encyclical, *Ecclesia de Eucharistia*,[9] in which he left us a sure magisterial statement of the Church's teaching on the Eucharist and a final testimony of the central place that this divine sacrament had in his own life.

The purpose of this Exhortation

5. This Post-Synodal Apostolic Exhortation seeks to take up the richness and variety of the reflections and proposals which emerged from the recent Ordinary General Assembly of the Synod of Bishops—from the *Lineamenta* to the *Propositiones*, along the way of the *Instrumentum*

Laboris, the *Relationes ante* and *post disceptationem*, the interventions of the Synod Fathers, the *auditores* and the fraternal delegates—and to offer some basic directions aimed at a renewed commitment to eucharistic enthusiasm and fervor in the Church. Conscious of the immense patrimony of doctrine and discipline accumulated over the centuries with regard to this sacrament,[10] I wish here to endorse the wishes expressed by the Synod Fathers[11] by encouraging the Christian people to deepen their understanding of the relationship between the *eucharistic mystery*, the *liturgical action*, and the *new spiritual worship* which derives from the Eucharist as the *sacrament of charity*. Consequently, I wish to set the present Exhortation alongside my first Encyclical Letter, *Deus Caritas Est*, in which I frequently mentioned the sacrament of the Eucharist and stressed its relationship to Christian love, both of God and of neighbor: "God incarnate draws us all to himself. We can thus understand how *agape* also became a term for the Eucharist: there God's own *agape* comes to us bodily, in order to continue his work in us and through us."[12]

PART I

The Eucharist, a Mystery to Be Believed

*"This is the work of God: that you believe
in him whom he has sent" (Jn 6:29).*

The Church's eucharistic faith

6. *"The mystery of faith!"* With these words, spoken immediately after the words of consecration, the priest proclaims the mystery being celebrated and expresses his wonder before the substantial change of bread and wine into the body and blood of the Lord Jesus, a reality which surpasses all human understanding. The Eucharist is a "mystery of faith" par excellence: "the sum and summary of our faith."[13] The Church's faith is essentially a eucharistic faith, and it is especially nourished at the table of the Eucharist. Faith and the sacraments are two complementary aspects of ecclesial life. Awakened by the preaching of God's word, faith is nourished and grows in the grace-filled encounter with the Risen Lord which takes place in the sacraments: "faith is expressed in the rite, while the rite reinforces and strengthens faith."[14] For this reason, the Sacrament of the Altar is always at the heart of the Church's life: "thanks to the Eucharist, the Church is reborn ever anew!"[15] The more lively the eucharistic faith of the People of God, the deeper is its sharing in ecclesial life in steadfast commitment to the mission entrusted by Christ to his disciples. The Church's very history bears witness to this. Every great reform has in some way been linked to the rediscovery of belief in the Lord's eucharistic presence among his people.

THE BLESSED TRINITY AND THE EUCHARIST

The bread come down from heaven

7. The first element of eucharistic faith is the mystery of God himself, trinitarian love. In Jesus' dialogue with Nicodemus, we find an illuminating expression in this regard: "God so loved the world that he gave his only Son, that whoever believes in him should not perish but have eternal life. For God sent the Son into the world, not to condemn the world, but that the world might be saved through him" (Jn 3:16-17). These words show the deepest source of God's gift. In the Eucharist Jesus does not give us a "thing," but himself; he offers his own body and pours out his own blood. He thus gives us the totality of his life and reveals the ultimate origin of this love. He is the eternal Son, given to us by the Father. In the Gospel we hear how Jesus, after feeding the crowds by multiplying the loaves and fishes, says to those who had followed him to the synagogue of Capernaum: "My Father gives you the true bread from heaven; for the bread of God is he who comes down from heaven, and gives life to the world" (Jn 6:32-33), and even identifies himself, his own flesh and blood, with that bread: "I am the living bread which came down from heaven; if anyone eats of this bread, he will live forever; and the bread which I shall give for the life of the world is my flesh" (Jn 6:51). Jesus thus shows that he is the bread of life which the eternal Father gives to mankind.

A free gift of the Blessed Trinity

8. The Eucharist reveals the loving plan that guides all of salvation history (cf. *Eph* 1:10; 3:8-11). There the *Deus Trinitas*, who is essentially love (cf. *1 Jn* 4:7-8), becomes fully a part of our human condition. In the bread and wine under whose appearances Christ gives himself to us in the paschal meal (cf. *Lk* 22:14-20; *1 Cor* 11:23-26), God's whole life encounters us and is sacramentally shared with us. God is a perfect communion of love between Father, Son and Holy Spirit. At creation itself, man was called to have some share in God's breath of life (cf. *Gen* 2:7). But it is in Christ, dead and risen, and in the outpouring of the Holy Spirit, given without measure (cf. *Jn* 3:34), that we have become

sharers of God's inmost life.[16] Jesus Christ, who "through the eternal Spirit offered himself without blemish to God" (*Heb* 9:14), makes us, in the gift of the Eucharist, sharers in God's own life. This is an absolutely free gift, the superabundant fulfillment of God's promises. The Church receives, celebrates and adores this gift in faithful obedience. The "mystery of faith" is thus a mystery of trinitarian love, a mystery in which we are called by grace to participate. We too should therefore exclaim with Saint Augustine: "If you see love, you see the Trinity."[17]

THE EUCHARIST: JESUS THE TRUE SACRIFICIAL LAMB

The new and eternal covenant in the blood of the Lamb

9. The mission for which Jesus came among us was accomplished in the Paschal Mystery. On the Cross from which he draws all people to himself (cf. *Jn* 12:32), just before "giving up the Spirit," he utters the words: "it is finished" (*Jn* 19:30). In the mystery of Christ's obedience unto death, even death on a Cross (cf. *Phil* 2:8), the new and eternal covenant was brought about. In his crucified flesh, God's freedom and our human freedom met definitively in an inviolable, eternally valid pact. Human sin was also redeemed once for all by God's Son (cf. *Heb* 7:27; *1 Jn* 2:2; 4:10). As I have said elsewhere, "Christ's death on the Cross is the culmination of that turning of God against himself in which he gives himself in order to raise man up and save him. This is love in its most radical form."[18] In the Paschal Mystery, our deliverance from evil and death has taken place. In instituting the Eucharist, Jesus had spoken of the "new and eternal covenant" in the shedding of his blood (cf. *Mt* 26:28; *Mk* 14:24; *Lk* 22:20). This, the ultimate purpose of his mission, was clear from the very beginning of his public life. Indeed, when, on the banks of the Jordan, John the Baptist saw Jesus coming towards him, he cried out: "Behold, the Lamb of God, who takes away the sin of the world" (*Jn* 1:29). It is significant that these same words are repeated at every celebration of Holy Mass, when the priest invites us to approach the altar: "This is *the Lamb of God* who

takes away the sins of the world. Happy are those who are called to his supper." Jesus is the *true* paschal lamb who freely gave himself in sacrifice for us, and thus brought about the new and eternal covenant. The Eucharist contains this radical newness, which is offered to us again at every celebration.[19]

The institution of the Eucharist

10. This leads us to reflect on the institution of the Eucharist at the Last Supper. It took place within a ritual meal commemorating the foundational event of the people of Israel: their deliverance from slavery in Egypt. This ritual meal, which called for the sacrifice of lambs (cf. *Ex* 12:1-28, 43-51), was a remembrance of the past, but at the same time a prophetic remembrance, the proclamation of a deliverance yet to come. The people had come to realize that their earlier liberation was not definitive, for their history continued to be marked by slavery and sin. The remembrance of their ancient liberation thus expanded to the invocation and expectation of a yet more profound, radical, universal and definitive salvation. This is the context in which Jesus introduces the newness of his gift. In the prayer of praise, the *Berakah*, he does not simply thank the Father for the great events of past history, but also for his own "exaltation." In instituting the sacrament of the Eucharist, Jesus anticipates and makes present the sacrifice of the Cross and the victory of the resurrection. At the same time, he reveals that he himself is the *true* sacrificial lamb, destined in the Father's plan from the foundation of the world, as we read in *The First Letter of Peter* (cf. 1:18-20). By placing his gift in this context, Jesus shows the salvific meaning of his death and resurrection, a mystery which renews history and the whole cosmos. The institution of the Eucharist demonstrates how Jesus' death, for all its violence and absurdity, became in him a supreme act of love and mankind's definitive deliverance from evil.

Figura transit in veritatem

11. Jesus thus brings his own radical *novum* to the ancient Hebrew sacrificial meal. For us Christians, that meal no longer need be repeated. As the Church Fathers rightly say, *figura transit in veritatem*:

the foreshadowing has given way to the truth itself. The ancient rite has been brought to fulfillment and definitively surpassed by the loving gift of the incarnate Son of God. The food of truth, Christ sacrificed for our sake, *dat figuris terminum*.[20] By his command to "do this in remembrance of me" (*Lk* 22:19; *1 Cor* 11:25), he asks us to respond to his gift and to make it sacramentally present. In these words the Lord expresses, as it were, his expectation that the Church, born of his sacrifice, will receive this gift, developing under the guidance of the Holy Spirit the liturgical form of the sacrament. The remembrance of his perfect gift consists not in the mere repetition of the Last Supper, but in the Eucharist itself, that is, in the radical newness of Christian worship. In this way, Jesus left us the task of entering into his "hour." "The Eucharist draws us into Jesus' act of self-oblation. More than just statically receiving the incarnate *Logos*, we enter into the very dynamic of his self-giving."[21] Jesus "draws us into himself."[22] The substantial conversion of bread and wine into his body and blood introduces within creation the principle of a radical change, a sort of "nuclear fission," to use an image familiar to us today, which penetrates to the heart of all being, a change meant to set off a process which transforms reality, a process leading ultimately to the transfiguration of the entire world, to the point where God will be all in all (cf. *1 Cor* 15:28).

THE HOLY SPIRIT AND THE EUCHARIST

Jesus and the Holy Spirit

12. With his word and with the elements of bread and wine, the Lord himself has given us the essentials of this new worship. The Church, his Bride, is called to celebrate the eucharistic banquet daily in his memory. She thus makes the redeeming sacrifice of her Bridegroom a part of human history and makes it sacramentally present in every culture. This great mystery is celebrated in the liturgical forms which the Church, guided by the Holy Spirit, develops in time and space.[23] We need a renewed awareness of the decisive role played by the Holy Spirit in the evolution of the liturgical form and the deepening

understanding of the sacred mysteries. The Paraclete, Christ's first gift to those who believe,[24] already at work in Creation (cf. *Gen* 1:2), is fully present throughout the life of the incarnate Word: Jesus Christ is conceived by the Virgin Mary by the power of the Holy Spirit (cf. *Mt* 1:18; *Lk* 1:35); at the beginning of his public mission, on the banks of the Jordan, he sees the Spirit descend upon him in the form of a dove (cf. *Mt* 3:16 and parallels); he acts, speaks and rejoices in the Spirit (cf. *Lk* 10:21), and he can offer himself in the Spirit (cf. *Heb* 9:14). In the so-called "farewell discourse" reported by John, Jesus clearly relates the gift of his life in the paschal mystery to the gift of the Spirit to his own (cf. *Jn* 16:7). Once risen, bearing in his flesh the signs of the passion, he can pour out the Spirit upon them (cf. *Jn* 20:22), making them sharers in his own mission (cf. *Jn* 20:21). The Spirit would then teach the disciples all things and bring to their remembrance all that Christ had said (cf. *Jn* 14:26), since it falls to him, as the Spirit of truth (cf. *Jn* 15:26), to guide the disciples into all truth (cf. *Jn* 16:13). In the account in *Acts*, the Spirit descends on the Apostles gathered in prayer with Mary on the day of Pentecost (cf. 2:1-4) and stirs them to undertake the mission of proclaiming the Good News to all peoples. Thus it is through the working of the Spirit that Christ himself continues to be present and active in his Church, starting with her vital center which is the Eucharist.

The Holy Spirit and the eucharistic celebration

13. Against this backdrop we can understand the decisive role played by the Holy Spirit in the eucharistic celebration, particularly with regard to transubstantiation. An awareness of this is clearly evident in the Fathers of the Church. Saint Cyril of Jerusalem, in his *Catecheses*, states that we "call upon God in his mercy to send his Holy Spirit upon the offerings before us, to transform the bread into the body of Christ and the wine into the blood of Christ. Whatever the Holy Spirit touches is sanctified and completely transformed."[25] Saint John Chrysostom too notes that the priest invokes the Holy Spirit when he celebrates the sacrifice:[26] like Elijah, the minister calls down the Holy Spirit so that "as grace comes down upon the victim, the souls of all are thereby inflamed."[27] The

spiritual life of the faithful can benefit greatly from a better appreciation of the richness of the anaphora: along with the words spoken by Christ at the Last Supper, it contains the epiclesis, the petition to the Father to send down the gift of the Spirit so that the bread and the wine will become the body and blood of Jesus Christ and that "the community as a whole will become ever more the body of Christ."[28] The Spirit invoked by the celebrant upon the gifts of bread and wine placed on the altar is the same Spirit who gathers the faithful "into one body" and makes of them a spiritual offering pleasing to the Father.[29]

THE EUCHARIST AND THE CHURCH

The Eucharist, causal principle of the Church

14. Through the sacrament of the Eucharist Jesus draws the faithful into his "hour"; he shows us the bond that he willed to establish between himself and us, between his own person and the Church. Indeed, in the sacrifice of the Cross, Christ gave birth to the Church as his Bride and his body. The Fathers of the Church often meditated on the relationship between Eve's coming forth from the side of Adam as he slept (cf. *Gen* 2:21-23) and the coming forth of the new Eve, the Church, from the open side of Christ sleeping in death: from Christ's pierced side, John recounts, there came forth blood and water (cf. *Jn* 19:34), the symbol of the sacraments.[30] A contemplative gaze "upon him whom they have pierced" (*Jn* 19:37) leads us to reflect on the causal connection between Christ's sacrifice, the Eucharist and the Church. The Church "draws her life from the Eucharist."[31] Since the Eucharist makes present Christ's redeeming sacrifice, we must start by acknowledging that "there is a causal influence of the Eucharist at the Church's very origins."[32] The Eucharist is Christ who gives himself to us and continually builds us up as his body. Hence, in the striking interplay between the Eucharist which builds up the Church, and the Church herself which "makes" the Eucharist,[33] the primary causality is expressed in the first formula: the Church is able to celebrate and adore the mystery of Christ present in the Eucharist precisely because

Christ first gave himself to her in the sacrifice of the Cross. The Church's ability to "make" the Eucharist is completely rooted in Christ's self-gift to her. Here we can see more clearly the meaning of Saint John's words: "he first loved us" (1 Jn 4:19). We too, at every celebration of the Eucharist, confess the primacy of Christ's gift. The causal influence of the Eucharist at the Church's origins definitively discloses both the chronological and ontological priority of the fact that it was Christ who loved us "first." For all eternity he remains the one who loves us first.

The Eucharist and ecclesial communion

15. The Eucharist is thus constitutive of the Church's being and activity. This is why Christian antiquity used the same words, *Corpus Christi*, to designate Christ's body born of the Virgin Mary, his eucharistic body and his ecclesial body.[34] This clear datum of the tradition helps us to appreciate the inseparability of Christ and the Church. The Lord Jesus, by offering himself in sacrifice for us, in his gift effectively pointed to the mystery of the Church. It is significant that the Second Eucharistic Prayer, invoking the Paraclete, formulates its prayer for the unity of the Church as follows: "*may all of us who share in the body and blood of Christ be brought together in unity by the Holy Spirit.*" These words help us to see clearly how the *res* of the sacrament of the Eucharist is the unity of the faithful within ecclesial communion. The Eucharist is thus found at the root of the Church as a mystery of communion.[35]

The relationship between Eucharist and *communio* had already been pointed out by the Servant of God John Paul II in his Encyclical *Ecclesia de Eucharistia*. He spoke of the memorial of Christ as "the supreme sacramental manifestation of communion in the Church."[36] The unity of ecclesial communion is concretely manifested in the Christian communities and is renewed at the celebration of the Eucharist, which unites them and differentiates them in the particular Churches, "*in quibus et ex quibus una et unica Ecclesia catholica exsistit.*"[37] The fact that the one Eucharist is celebrated in each Diocese around its own Bishop helps us to see how those particular Churches subsist *in* and *ex Ecclesia*. Indeed, "the oneness and indivisibility of the eucharistic body of the Lord implies the oneness of his mystical body, which is the one and indivisible Church. From the eucharistic center arises the necessary openness of every celebrating community, of every particular Church. By allowing itself to be drawn into the open arms of the Lord, it achieves insertion into his one and undivided body."[38] Consequently, in the celebration of the Eucharist, the individual members of the faithful find themselves in *their* Church, that is, in the Church of Christ. From this eucharistic perspective, adequately understood, ecclesial communion is seen to be catholic by its very nature.[39] An emphasis on this eucharistic basis of ecclesial communion can also contribute greatly to the ecumenical dialogue with the Churches and Ecclesial Communities which are not in full communion with the See of Peter. The Eucharist objectively creates a powerful bond of unity between the Catholic Church and the Orthodox Churches, which have preserved the authentic and integral nature of the eucharistic mystery. At the same time, emphasis on the ecclesial character of the Eucharist can become an important element of the dialogue with the Communities of the Reformed tradition.[40]

THE EUCHARIST AND THE SACRAMENTS

The sacramentality of the Church
16. The Second Vatican Council recalled that "all the sacraments, and indeed all ecclesiastical ministries and works of the apostolate, are bound up with the Eucharist and are directed towards it. For in the most blessed Eucharist is contained the entire spiritual wealth of the Church, namely Christ himself our Pasch and our living bread, who gives life to humanity through his flesh—that flesh which is given life and gives life by the Holy Spirit. Thus men and women are invited and led to offer themselves, their works and all creation in union with Christ."[41] This close relationship of the Eucharist with the other sacraments and the Christian life can be most fully understood when we contemplate the mystery of the Church herself as a sacrament.[42] The Council in this regard stated that "the Church, in Christ, is a sacrament—a sign and instrument—of communion with God and of

the unity of the entire human race."[43] To quote Saint Cyprian, as "a people made one by the unity of the Father, the Son and the Holy Spirit,"[44] she is the sacrament of trinitarian communion.

The fact that the Church is the "universal sacrament of salvation"[45] shows how the sacramental economy ultimately determines the way that Christ, the one Savior, through the Spirit, reaches our lives in all their particularity. The Church *receives* and at the same time *expresses* what she herself is in the seven sacraments, thanks to which God's grace concretely influences the lives of the faithful, so that their whole existence, redeemed by Christ, can become an act of worship pleasing to God. From this perspective, I would like here to draw attention to some elements brought up by the Synod Fathers which may help us to grasp the relationship of each of the sacraments to the eucharistic mystery.

I. THE EUCHARIST AND CHRISTIAN INITIATION

The Eucharist, the fullness of Christian initiation

17. If the Eucharist is truly the source and summit of the Church's life and mission, it follows that the process of Christian initiation must constantly be directed to the reception of this sacrament. As the Synod Fathers said, we need to ask ourselves whether in our Christian communities the close link between Baptism, Confirmation and Eucharist is sufficiently recognized.[46] It must never be forgotten that our reception of Baptism and Confirmation is ordered to the Eucharist. Accordingly, our pastoral practice should reflect a more unitary understanding of the process of Christian initiation. The sacrament of Baptism, by which we were conformed to Christ,[47] incorporated in the Church and made children of God, is the portal to all the sacraments. It makes us part of the one Body of Christ (cf. *1 Cor* 12:13), a priestly people. Still, it is our participation in the Eucharistic sacrifice which perfects within us the gifts given to us at Baptism. The gifts of the Spirit are given for the building up of Christ's Body (*1 Cor* 12) and for ever greater witness to the Gospel in the world.[48] The Holy Eucharist,

then, brings Christian initiation to completion and represents the center and goal of all sacramental life.[49]

The order of the sacraments of initiation

18. In this regard, attention needs to be paid to the order of the sacraments of initiation. Different traditions exist within the Church. There is a clear variation between, on the one hand, the ecclesial customs of the East[50] and the practice of the West regarding the initiation of adults,[51] and, on the other hand, the procedure adopted for children.[52] Yet these variations are not properly of the dogmatic order, but are pastoral in character. Concretely, it needs to be seen which practice better enables the faithful to put the sacrament of the Eucharist at the center, as the goal of the whole process of initiation. In close collaboration with the competent offices of the Roman Curia, Bishops' Conferences should examine the effectiveness of current approaches to Christian initiation, so that the faithful can be helped both to mature through the formation received in our communities and to give their lives an authentically eucharistic direction, so that they can offer a reason for the hope within them in a way suited to our times (cf. 1 Pet 3:15).

Initiation, the ecclesial community and the family

19. It should be kept in mind that the whole of Christian initiation is a process of conversion undertaken with God's help and with constant reference to the ecclesial community, both when an adult is seeking entry into the Church, as happens in places of first evangelization and in many secularized regions, and when parents request the sacraments for their children. In this regard, I would like to call particular attention to the relationship between Christian initiation and the family. In pastoral work it is always important to make Christian families part of the process of initiation. Receiving Baptism, Confirmation and First Holy Communion are key moments not only for the individual receiving them but also for the entire family, which should be supported in its educational role by the various elements of the ecclesial community.[53] Here I would emphasize the importance of

First Holy Communion. For many of the faithful, this day continues to be memorable as the moment when, even if in a rudimentary way, they first came to understand the importance of a personal encounter with Jesus. Parish pastoral programs should make the most of this highly significant moment.

II. THE EUCHARIST AND THE
SACRAMENT OF RECONCILIATION

Their intrinsic relationship

20. The Synod Fathers rightly stated that a love for the Eucharist leads to a growing appreciation of the sacrament of Reconciliation.[54] Given the connection between these sacraments, an authentic catechesis on the meaning of the Eucharist must include the call to pursue the path of penance (cf. 1 Cor 11:27-29). We know that the faithful are surrounded by a culture that tends to eliminate the sense of sin[55] and to promote a superficial approach that overlooks the need to be in a state of grace in order to approach sacramental communion worthily.[56] The loss of a consciousness of sin always entails a certain superficiality in the understanding of God's love. Bringing out the elements within the rite of Mass that express consciousness of personal sin and, at the same time, of God's mercy, can prove most helpful to the faithful.[57] Furthermore, the relationship between the Eucharist and the sacrament of Reconciliation reminds us that sin is never a purely individual affair; it always damages the ecclesial communion that we have entered through Baptism. For this reason, Reconciliation, as the Fathers of the Church would say, is *laboriosus quidam baptismus*;[58] they thus emphasized that the outcome of the process of conversion is also the restoration of full ecclesial communion, expressed in a return to the Eucharist.[59]

Some pastoral concerns

21. The Synod recalled that Bishops have the pastoral duty of promoting within their Dioceses a reinvigorated catechesis on the conversion born of the Eucharist, and of encouraging frequent confession among

the faithful. All priests should dedicate themselves with generosity, commitment and competency to administering the sacrament of Reconciliation.[60] In this regard, it is important that the confessionals in our churches should be clearly visible expressions of the importance of this sacrament. I ask pastors to be vigilant with regard to the celebration of the sacrament of Reconciliation, and to limit the practice of general absolution exclusively to the cases permitted,[61] since individual absolution is the only form intended for ordinary use.[62] Given the need to rediscover sacramental forgiveness, there ought to be a *Penitentiary* in every Diocese.[63] Finally, a balanced and sound practice of gaining *indulgences*, whether for oneself or for the dead, can be helpful for a renewed appreciation of the relationship between the Eucharist and Reconciliation. By this means the faithful obtain "remission before God of the temporal punishment due to sins whose guilt has already been forgiven."[64] The use of indulgences helps us to understand that by our efforts alone we would be incapable of making reparation for the wrong we have done, and that the sins of each individual harm the whole community. Furthermore, the practice of indulgences, which involves not only the doctrine of Christ's infinite merits, but also that of the communion of the saints, reminds us "how closely we are united to each other in Christ . . . and how the supernatural life of each can help others."[65] Since the conditions for gaining an indulgence include going to confession and receiving sacramental communion, this practice can effectively sustain the faithful on their journey of conversion and in rediscovering the centrality of the Eucharist in the Christian life.

III. THE EUCHARIST AND THE ANOINTING OF THE SICK

22. Jesus did not only send his disciples forth to heal the sick (cf. *Mt* 10:8; *Lk* 9:2, 10:9); he also instituted a specific sacrament for them: the Anointing of the Sick.[66] The *Letter of James* attests to the presence of this sacramental sign in the early Christian community (cf. 5:14-16). If the Eucharist shows how Christ's sufferings and death have been transformed into love, the Anointing of the Sick, for its part, unites

the sick with Christ's self-offering for the salvation of all, so that they too, within the mystery of the communion of saints, can participate in the redemption of the world. The relationship between these two sacraments becomes clear in situations of serious illness: "In addition to the Anointing of the Sick, the Church offers those who are about to leave this life the Eucharist as viaticum."[67] On their journey to the Father, communion in the Body and Blood of Christ appears as the seed of eternal life and the power of resurrection: "Anyone who eats my flesh and drinks my blood has eternal life and I will raise him up on the last day" (Jn 6:54). Since viaticum gives the sick a glimpse of the fullness of the Paschal Mystery, its administration should be readily provided for.[68] Attentive pastoral care shown to those who are ill brings great spiritual benefit to the entire community, since whatever we do to one of the least of our brothers and sisters, we do to Jesus himself (cf. Mt 25:40).

IV. THE EUCHARIST AND THE
SACRAMENT OF HOLY ORDERS

In persona Christi capitis

23. The intrinsic relationship between the Eucharist and the sacrament of Holy Orders clearly emerges from Jesus' own words in the Upper Room: "Do this in memory of me" (Lk 22:19). On the night before he died, Jesus instituted the Eucharist and at the same time established the *priesthood of the New Covenant*. He is priest, victim and altar: the mediator between God the Father and his people (cf. Heb 5:5-10), the victim of atonement (cf. 1 Jn 2:2, 4:10) who offers himself on the altar of the Cross. No one can say "this is my body" and "this is the cup of my blood" except in the name and in the person of Christ, the one high priest of the new and eternal Covenant (cf. Heb 8-9). Earlier meetings of the Synod of Bishops had considered the question of the ordained priesthood, both with regard to the nature of the ministry[69] and the formation of candidates.[70] Here, in the light of the discussion that took place during the last Synod, I consider it important to recall

several important points about the relationship between the sacrament of the Eucharist and Holy Orders. First of all, we need to stress once again that the connection between *Holy Orders and the Eucharist* is seen most clearly at Mass, when the Bishop or priest presides *in the person of Christ the Head*.

The Church teaches that priestly ordination is the indispensable condition for the valid celebration of the Eucharist.[71] Indeed, "in the ecclesial service of the ordained minister, it is Christ himself who is present to his Church as Head of his Body, Shepherd of his flock, High Priest of the redemptive sacrifice."[72] Certainly the ordained minister also acts "in the name of the whole Church, when presenting to God the prayer of the Church, and above all when offering the eucharistic sacrifice."[73] As a result, priests should be conscious of the fact that in their ministry they must never put themselves or their personal opinions in first place, but Jesus Christ. Any attempt to make themselves the center of the liturgical action contradicts their very identity as priests. The priest is above all a servant of others, and he must continually work at being a sign pointing to Christ, a docile instrument in the Lord's hands. This is seen particularly in his humility in leading the liturgical assembly, in obedience to the rite, uniting himself to it in mind and heart, and avoiding anything that might give the impression of an inordinate emphasis on his own personality. I encourage the clergy always to see their eucharistic ministry as a humble service offered to Christ and his Church. The priesthood, as Saint Augustine said, is *amoris officium*,[74] it is the office of the good shepherd, who offers his life for his sheep (cf. Jn 10:14-15).

The Eucharist and priestly celibacy

24. The Synod Fathers wished to emphasize that the ministerial priesthood, through ordination, calls for complete configuration to Christ. While respecting the different practice and tradition of the Eastern Churches, there is a need to reaffirm the profound meaning of priestly celibacy, which is rightly considered a priceless treasure, and is also confirmed by the Eastern practice of choosing Bishops only from the ranks of the celibate. These Churches also greatly esteem the

decision of many priests to embrace celibacy. This choice on the part of the priest expresses in a special way the dedication which conforms him to Christ and his exclusive offering of himself for the Kingdom of God.[75] The fact that Christ himself, the eternal priest, lived his mission even to the sacrifice of the Cross in the state of virginity constitutes the sure point of reference for understanding the meaning of the tradition of the Latin Church. It is not sufficient to understand priestly celibacy in purely functional terms. Celibacy is really a special way of conforming oneself to Christ's own way of life. This choice has first and foremost a nuptial meaning; it is a profound identification with the heart of Christ the Bridegroom who gives his life for his Bride. In continuity with the great ecclesial tradition, with the Second Vatican Council[76] and with my predecessors in the papacy,[77] I reaffirm the beauty and the importance of a priestly life lived in celibacy as a sign expressing total and exclusive devotion to Christ, to the Church and to the Kingdom of God, and I therefore confirm that it remains obligatory in the Latin tradition. Priestly celibacy lived with maturity, joy and dedication is an immense blessing for the Church and for society itself.

The clergy shortage and the pastoral care of vocations

25. In the light of the connection between the sacrament of Holy Orders and the Eucharist, the Synod considered the difficult situation that has arisen in various Dioceses which face a shortage of priests. This happens not only in some areas of first evangelization, but also in many countries of long-standing Christian tradition. Certainly a more equitable distribution of clergy would help to solve the problem. Efforts need to be made to encourage a greater awareness of this situation at every level. Bishops should involve Institutes of Consecrated Life and the new ecclesial groups in their pastoral needs, while respecting their particular charisms, and they should invite the clergy to become more open to serving the Church wherever there is need, even if this calls for sacrifice.[78] The Synod also discussed pastoral initiatives aimed at promoting, especially among the young, an attitude of interior openness to a priestly calling. The situation cannot be resolved by purely practical decisions. On no account should Bishops react to real

and understandable concerns about the shortage of priests by failing to carry out adequate vocational discernment, or by admitting to seminary formation and ordination candidates who lack the necessary qualities for priestly ministry.[79] An insufficiently formed clergy, admitted to ordination without the necessary discernment, will not easily be able to offer a witness capable of evoking in others the desire to respond generously to Christ's call. The pastoral care of vocations needs to involve the entire Christian community in every area of its life.[80] Obviously, this pastoral work on all levels also includes exploring the matter with families, which are often indifferent or even opposed to the idea of a priestly vocation. Families should generously embrace the gift of life and bring up their children to be open to doing God's will. In a word, they must have the courage to set before young people the radical decision to follow Christ, showing them how deeply rewarding it is.

Gratitude and hope

26. Finally, we need to have ever greater faith and hope in God's providence. Even if there is a shortage of priests in some areas, we must never lose confidence that Christ continues to inspire men to leave everything behind and to dedicate themselves totally to celebrating the sacred mysteries, preaching the Gospel and ministering to the flock. In this regard, I wish to express the gratitude of the whole Church for all those Bishops and priests who carry out their respective missions with fidelity, devotion and zeal. Naturally, the Church's gratitude also goes to deacons, who receive the laying on of hands "not for priesthood but for service."[81] As the Synod Assembly recommended, I offer a special word of thanks to those *Fidei Donum* priests who work faithfully and generously at building up the community by proclaiming the word of God and breaking the Bread of Life, devoting all their energy to serving the mission of the Church.[82] Let us thank God for all those priests who have suffered even to the sacrifice of their lives in order to serve Christ. The eloquence of their example shows what it means to be a priest to the end. Theirs is a moving witness that can inspire many young people to follow Christ and to expend their lives for others, and thus to discover true life.

V. THE EUCHARIST AND MATRIMONY

The Eucharist, a nuptial sacrament

27. The Eucharist, as the sacrament of charity, has a particular relationship with the love of man and woman united in marriage. A deeper understanding of this relationship is needed at the present time.[83] Pope John Paul II frequently spoke of the nuptial character of the Eucharist and its special relationship with the sacrament of Matrimony: "The Eucharist is the sacrament of our redemption. It is the sacrament of the Bridegroom and of the Bride."[84] Moreover, "the entire Christian life bears the mark of the spousal love of Christ and the Church. Already Baptism, the entry into the People of God, is a nuptial mystery; it is so to speak the nuptial bath which precedes the wedding feast, the Eucharist."[85] The Eucharist inexhaustibly strengthens the indissoluble unity and love of every Christian marriage. By the power of the sacrament, the marriage bond is intrinsically linked to the eucharistic unity of Christ the Bridegroom and his Bride, the Church (cf. *Eph* 5:31-32). The mutual consent that husband and wife exchange in Christ, which establishes them as a community of life and love, also has a eucharistic dimension. Indeed, in the theology of Saint Paul, conjugal love is a sacramental sign of Christ's love for his Church, a love culminating in the Cross, the expression of his "marriage" with humanity and at the same time the origin and heart of the Eucharist. For this reason the Church manifests her particular spiritual closeness to all those who have built their family on the sacrament of Matrimony.[86] The family—the domestic Church[87]—is a primary sphere of the Church's life, especially because of its decisive role in the Christian education of children.[88] In this context, the Synod also called for an acknowledgment of the unique mission of women in the family and in society, a mission that needs to be defended, protected and promoted.[89] Marriage and motherhood represent essential realities which must never be denigrated.

The Eucharist and the unicity of marriage

28. In the light of this intrinsic relationship between marriage, the family and the Eucharist, we can turn to several pastoral problems. The indissoluble, exclusive and faithful bond uniting Christ and the Church, which finds sacramental expression in the Eucharist, corresponds to the basic anthropological fact that man is meant to be definitively united to one woman and vice versa (cf. *Gen* 2:24, *Mt* 19:5). With this in mind, the Synod of Bishops addressed the question of pastoral practice regarding people who come to the Gospel from cultures in which polygamy is practiced. Those living in this situation who open themselves to Christian faith need to be helped to integrate their life-plan into the radical newness of Christ. During the catechumenate, Christ encounters them in their specific circumstances and calls them to embrace the full truth of love, making whatever sacrifices are necessary in order to arrive at perfect ecclesial communion. The Church accompanies them with a pastoral care that is gentle yet firm,[90] above all by showing them the light shed by the Christian mysteries on nature and on human affections.

The Eucharist and the indissolubility of marriage

29. If the Eucharist expresses the irrevocable nature of God's love in Christ for his Church, we can then understand why it implies, with regard to the sacrament of Matrimony, that indissolubility to which all true love necessarily aspires.[91] There was good reason for the pastoral attention that the Synod gave to the painful situations experienced by some of the faithful who, having celebrated the sacrament of Matrimony, then divorced and remarried. This represents a complex and troubling pastoral problem, a real scourge for contemporary society, and one which increasingly affects the Catholic community as well. The Church's pastors, out of love for the truth, are obliged to discern different situations carefully, in order to be able to offer appropriate spiritual guidance to the faithful involved.[92] The Synod of Bishops confirmed the Church's practice, based on Sacred Scripture (cf. *Mk* 10:2-12), of not admitting the divorced and remarried to the sacraments, since their state and their condition of life objectively

contradict the loving union of Christ and the Church signified and made present in the Eucharist. Yet the divorced and remarried continue to belong to the Church, which accompanies them with special concern and encourages them to live as fully as possible the Christian life through regular participation at Mass, albeit without receiving communion, listening to the word of God, eucharistic adoration, prayer, participation in the life of the community, honest dialogue with a priest or spiritual director, dedication to the life of charity, works of penance, and commitment to the education of their children.

When legitimate doubts exist about the validity of the prior sacramental marriage, the necessary investigation must be carried out to establish if these are well-founded. Consequently there is a need to ensure, in full respect for canon law,[93] the presence of local ecclesiastical tribunals, their pastoral character, and their correct and prompt functioning.[94] Each Diocese should have a sufficient number of persons with the necessary preparation, so that the ecclesiastical tribunals can operate in an expeditious manner. I repeat that "it is a grave obligation to bring the Church's institutional activity in her tribunals ever closer to the faithful."[95] At the same time, pastoral care must not be understood as if it were somehow in conflict with the law. Rather, one should begin by assuming that the fundamental point of encounter between the law and pastoral care is *love for the truth*: truth is never something purely abstract, but "a real part of the human and Christian journey of every member of the faithful."[96] Finally, where the nullity of the marriage bond is not declared and objective circumstances make it impossible to cease cohabitation, the Church encourages these members of the faithful to commit themselves to living their relationship in fidelity to the demands of God's law, as friends, as brother and sister; in this way they will be able to return to the table of the Eucharist, taking care to observe the Church's established and approved practice in this regard. This path, if it is to be possible and fruitful, must be supported by pastors and by adequate ecclesial initiatives, nor can it ever involve the blessing of these relations, lest confusion arise among the faithful concerning the value of marriage.[97]

26

Given the complex cultural context which the Church today encounters in many countries, the Synod also recommended devoting maximum pastoral attention to training couples preparing for marriage and to ascertaining beforehand their convictions regarding the obligations required for the validity of the sacrament of Matrimony. Serious discernment in this matter will help to avoid situations where impulsive decisions or superficial reasons lead two young people to take on responsibilities that they are then incapable of honoring.[98] The good that the Church and society as a whole expect from marriage and from the family founded upon marriage is so great as to call for full pastoral commitment to this particular area. Marriage and the family are institutions that must be promoted and defended from every possible misrepresentation of their true nature, since whatever is injurious to them is injurious to society itself.

THE EUCHARIST AND ESCHATOLOGY

The Eucharist: A gift to men and women on their journey
30. If it is true that the sacraments are part of the Church's pilgrimage through history[99] towards the full manifestation of the victory of the risen Christ, it is also true that, especially in the liturgy of the Eucharist, they give us a real foretaste of the eschatological fulfillment for which every human being and all creation are destined (cf. *Rom* 8:19ff.). Man is created for that true and eternal happiness which only God's love can give. But our wounded freedom would go astray were it not already able to experience something of that future fulfillment. Moreover, to move forward in the right direction, we all need to be guided towards our final goal. That goal is Christ himself, the Lord who conquered sin and death, and who makes himself present to us in a special way in the eucharistic celebration. Even though we remain "aliens and exiles" in this world (*1 Pet* 2:11), through faith we already share in the fullness of risen life. The eucharistic banquet, by disclosing its powerful eschatological dimension, comes to the aid of our freedom as we continue our journey.

The eschatological banquet

31. Reflecting on this mystery, we can say that Jesus' coming responded to an expectation present in the people of Israel, in the whole of humanity and ultimately in creation itself. By his self-gift, he objectively inaugurated the eschatological age. Christ came to gather together the scattered People of God (cf. *Jn* 11:52) and clearly manifested his intention to gather together the community of the covenant, in order to bring to fulfillment the promises made by God to the fathers of old (cf. *Jer* 23:3; *Lk* 1:55, 70). In the calling of the Twelve, which is to be understood in relation to the twelve tribes of Israel, and in the command he gave them at the Last Supper, before his redemptive passion, to celebrate his memorial, Jesus showed that he wished to transfer to the entire community which he had founded the task of being, within history, the sign and instrument of the eschatological gathering that had its origin in him. Consequently, every eucharistic celebration sacramentally accomplishes the eschatological gathering of the People of God. For us, the eucharistic banquet is a real foretaste of the final banquet foretold by the prophets (cf. *Is* 25:6-9) and described in the New Testament as "the marriage-feast of the Lamb" (*Rev* 19:7-9), to be celebrated in the joy of the communion of saints.[100]

Prayer for the dead

32. The eucharistic celebration, in which we proclaim that Christ has died and risen, and will come again, is a pledge of the future glory in which our bodies too will be glorified. Celebrating the memorial of our salvation strengthens our hope in the resurrection of the body and in the possibility of meeting once again, face to face, those who have gone before us marked with the sign of faith. In this context, I wish, together with the Synod Fathers, to remind all the faithful of the importance of prayers for the dead, especially the offering of Mass for them, so that, once purified, they can come to the beatific vision of God.[101] A rediscovery of the eschatological dimension inherent in the Eucharist, celebrated and adored, will help sustain us on our journey and comfort us in the hope of glory (cf. *Rom* 5:2; *Tit* 2:13).

THE EUCHARIST AND THE VIRGIN MARY

33. From the relationship between the Eucharist and the individual sacraments, and from the eschatological significance of the sacred mysteries, the overall shape of the Christian life emerges, a life called at all times to be an act of spiritual worship, a self-offering pleasing to God. Although we are all still journeying towards the complete fulfillment of our hope, this does not mean that we cannot already gratefully acknowledge that God's gifts to us have found their perfect fulfillment in the Virgin Mary, Mother of God and our Mother. Mary's Assumption body and soul into heaven is for us a sign of sure hope, for it shows us, on our pilgrimage through time, the eschatological goal of which the sacrament of the Eucharist enables us even now to have a foretaste.

In Mary most holy, we also see perfectly fulfilled the "sacramental" way that God comes down to meet his creatures and involves them in his saving work. From the Annunciation to Pentecost, Mary of Nazareth appears as someone whose freedom is completely open to God's will. Her immaculate conception is revealed precisely in her unconditional docility to God's word. Obedient faith in response to God's work shapes her life at every moment. A virgin attentive to God's word, she lives in complete harmony with his will; she treasures in her heart the words that come to her from God and, piecing them together like a mosaic, she learns to understand them more deeply (cf. *Lk* 2:19, 51); Mary is the great Believer who places herself confidently in God's hands, abandoning herself to his will.[102] This mystery deepens as she becomes completely involved in the redemptive mission of Jesus. In the words of the Second Vatican Council, "the blessed Virgin advanced in her pilgrimage of faith, and faithfully persevered in her union with her Son until she stood at the Cross, in keeping with the divine plan (cf. *Jn* 19:25), suffering deeply with her only-begotten Son, associating herself with his sacrifice in her mother's heart, and lovingly consenting to the immolation of the victim who was born of her. Finally, she was given by the same Christ Jesus, dying on the Cross, as a mother to his disciple, with these words: 'Woman, behold your Son.'"[103] From the Annunciation to the Cross, Mary is the one who received the Word, made flesh within her and then silenced in death. It is she, lastly, who took into her arms the lifeless body of the one who truly loved his own "to the end" (*Jn* 13:1).

Consequently, every time we approach the Body and Blood of Christ in the eucharistic liturgy, we also turn to her who, by her complete fidelity, received Christ's sacrifice for the whole Church. The Synod Fathers rightly declared that "Mary inaugurates the Church's participation in the sacrifice of the Redeemer."[104] She is the Immaculata, who receives God's gift unconditionally and is thus associated with his work of salvation. Mary of Nazareth, icon of the nascent Church, is the model for each of us, called to receive the gift that Jesus makes of himself in the Eucharist.

PART II

The Eucharist, a Mystery
to Be Celebrated

"Truly, truly, I say to you, it was not Moses who
gave you the bread from heaven; my Father gives
you the true bread from heaven" (*Jn* 6:32).

Lex orandi *and* lex credendi

34. The Synod of Bishops reflected at length on the intrinsic
relationship between eucharistic faith and eucharistic celebration,
pointing out the connection between the *lex orandi* and the *lex credendi*,
and stressing the primacy of the *liturgical action*. The Eucharist should
be experienced as a mystery of faith, celebrated authentically and with
a clear awareness that "the *intellectus fidei* has a primordial relationship
to the Church's liturgical action."[105] Theological reflection in this
area can never prescind from the sacramental order instituted by
Christ himself. On the other hand, the liturgical action can never be
considered generically, prescinding from the mystery of faith. Our faith
and the eucharistic liturgy both have their source in the same event:
Christ's gift of himself in the Paschal Mystery.

Beauty and the liturgy

35. This relationship between creed and worship is evidenced in a
particular way by the rich theological and liturgical category of beauty.
Like the rest of Christian Revelation, the liturgy is inherently linked
to beauty: it is *veritatis splendor*. The liturgy is a radiant expression of
the paschal mystery, in which Christ draws us to himself and calls us to
communion. As Saint Bonaventure would say, in Jesus we contemplate
beauty and splendor at their source.[106] This is no mere aestheticism, but
the concrete way in which the truth of God's love in Christ encounters
us, attracts us and delights us, enabling us to emerge from ourselves

and drawing us towards our true vocation, which is love.[107] God allows himself to be glimpsed first in creation, in the beauty and harmony of the cosmos (cf. *Wis* 13:5; *Rom* 1:19-20). In the Old Testament we see many signs of the grandeur of God's power as he manifests his glory in his wondrous deeds among the Chosen People (cf. *Ex* 14; 16:10; 24:12-18; *Num* 14:20-23). In the New Testament this epiphany of beauty reaches definitive fulfillment in God's revelation in Jesus Christ:[108] Christ is the full manifestation of the glory of God. In the glorification of the Son, the Father's glory shines forth and is communicated (cf. *Jn* 1:14; 8:54; 12:28; 17:1). Yet this beauty is not simply a harmony of proportion and form; "the fairest of the sons of men" (*Ps* 45[44]:3) is also, mysteriously, the one "who had no form or comeliness that we should look at him, and no beauty that we should desire him" (*Is* 53:2). Jesus Christ shows us how the truth of love can transform even the dark mystery of death into the radiant light of the resurrection. Here the splendor of God's glory surpasses all worldly beauty. The truest beauty is the love of God, who definitively revealed himself to us in the paschal mystery.

The beauty of the liturgy is part of this mystery; it is a sublime expression of God's glory and, in a certain sense, a glimpse of heaven on earth. The memorial of Jesus' redemptive sacrifice contains something of that beauty which Peter, James and John beheld when the Master, making his way to Jerusalem, was transfigured before their eyes (cf. *Mk* 9:2). Beauty, then, is not mere decoration, but rather an essential element of the liturgical action, since it is an attribute of God himself and his revelation. These considerations should make us realize the care which is needed, if the liturgical action is to reflect its innate splendor.

THE EUCHARISTIC CELEBRATION,
THE WORK OF *"CHRISTUS TOTUS"*

Christus totus in capite et in corpore

36. The "subject" of the liturgy's intrinsic beauty is Christ himself, risen and glorified in the Holy Spirit, who includes the Church in his

work.[109] Here we can recall an evocative phrase of Saint Augustine which strikingly describes this dynamic of faith proper to the Eucharist. The great Bishop of Hippo, speaking specifically of the eucharistic mystery, stresses the fact that Christ assimilates us to himself: "The bread you see on the altar, sanctified by the word of God, is the body of Christ. The chalice, or rather, what the chalice contains, sanctified by the word of God, is the blood of Christ. In these signs, Christ the Lord willed to entrust to us his body and the blood which he shed for the forgiveness of our sins. If you have received them properly, you yourselves are what you have received."[110] Consequently, "not only have we become Christians, we have become Christ himself."[111] We can thus contemplate God's mysterious work, which brings about a profound unity between ourselves and the Lord Jesus: "one should not believe that Christ is in the head but not in the body; rather he is complete in the head and in the body."[112]

The Eucharist and the risen Christ

37. Since the eucharistic liturgy is essentially an *actio Dei* which draws us into Christ through the Holy Spirit, its basic structure is not something within our power to change, nor can it be held hostage by the latest trends. Here too Saint Paul's irrefutable statement applies: "no one can lay any foundation other than the one that has been laid, which is Jesus Christ" (*1 Cor* 3:11). Again it is the Apostle of the Gentiles who assures us that, with regard to the Eucharist, he is presenting not his own teaching but what he himself has received (cf. *1 Cor* 11:23). The celebration of the Eucharist implies and involves the living Tradition. The Church celebrates the eucharistic sacrifice in obedience to Christ's command, based on her experience of the Risen Lord and the outpouring of the Holy Spirit. For this reason, from the beginning, the Christian community has gathered for the *fractio panis* on the Lord's Day. Sunday, the day Christ rose from the dead, is also the first day of the week, the day which the Old Testament tradition saw as the beginning of God's work of creation. The day of creation has now become the day of the "new creation," the day of our liberation, when we commemorate Christ who died and rose again.[113]

38. In the course of the Synod, there was frequent insistence on the need to avoid any antithesis between the *ars celebrandi*, the art of proper celebration, and the full, active and fruitful participation of all the faithful. The primary way to foster the participation of the People of God in the sacred rite is the proper celebration of the rite itself. The *ars celebrandi* is the best way to ensure their *actuosa participatio*.[114] The *ars celebrandi* is the fruit of faithful adherence to the liturgical norms in all their richness; indeed, for two thousand years this way of celebrating has sustained the faith life of all believers, called to take part in the celebration as the People of God, a royal priesthood, a holy nation (cf. *1 Pet* 2:4-5, 9).[115]

The Bishop, celebrant par excellence

39. While it is true that the whole People of God participates in the eucharistic liturgy, a correct *ars celebrandi* necessarily entails a specific responsibility on the part of those who have received the sacrament of Holy Orders. Bishops, priests, and deacons, each according to his proper rank, must consider the celebration of the liturgy as their principal duty.[116] Above all, this is true of the Diocesan Bishop: as "the chief steward of the mysteries of God in the particular Church entrusted to his care, he is the moderator, promoter, and guardian of the whole of its liturgical life."[117] This is essential for the life of the particular Church, not only because communion with the Bishop is required for the lawfulness of every celebration within his territory, but also because he himself is the celebrant par excellence within his Diocese.[118] It is his responsibility to ensure unity and harmony in the celebrations taking place in his territory. Consequently the Bishop must be "determined that the priests, the deacons, and the lay Christian faithful grasp ever more deeply the genuine meaning of the rites and liturgical texts, and thereby be led to an active and fruitful celebration of the Eucharist."[119] I would ask that every effort be made to ensure that the liturgies which the Bishop celebrates in his Cathedral are carried out with complete

respect for the *ars celebrandi*, so that they can be considered an example for the entire Diocese.[120]

Respect for the liturgical books and the richness of signs

40. Emphasizing the importance of the *ars celebrandi* also leads to an appreciation of the value of the liturgical norms.[121] The *ars celebrandi* should foster a sense of the sacred and the use of outward signs which help to cultivate this sense, such as, for example, the harmony of the rite, the liturgical vestments, the furnishings and the sacred space. The eucharistic celebration is enhanced when priests and liturgical leaders are committed to making known the current liturgical texts and norms, making available the great riches found in the *General Instruction of the Roman Missal* and the *Order of Readings for Mass*. Perhaps we take it for granted that our ecclesial communities already know and appreciate these resources, but this is not always the case. These texts contain riches which have preserved and expressed the faith and experience of the People of God over its two-thousand-year history. Equally important for a correct *ars celebrandi* is an attentiveness to the various kinds of language that the liturgy employs: words and music, gestures and silence, movement, the liturgical colors of the vestments. By its very nature the liturgy operates on different levels of communication which enable it to engage the whole human person. The simplicity of its gestures and the sobriety of its orderly sequence of signs communicate and inspire more than any contrived and inappropriate additions. Attentiveness and fidelity to the specific structure of the rite express both a recognition of the nature of Eucharist as a gift and, on the part of the minister, a docile openness to receiving this ineffable gift.

Art at the service of the liturgy

41. The profound connection between beauty and the liturgy should make us attentive to every work of art placed at the service of the celebration.[122] Certainly an important element of sacred art is church architecture,[123] which should highlight the unity of the furnishings of the sanctuary, such as the altar, the crucifix, the tabernacle, the ambo

and the celebrant's chair. Here it is important to remember that the purpose of sacred architecture is to offer the Church a fitting space for the celebration of the mysteries of faith, especially the Eucharist.[124] The very nature of a Christian church is defined by the liturgy, which is an assembly of the faithful (*ecclesia*) who are the living stones of the Church (cf. *1 Pet* 2:5).

This same principle holds true for sacred art in general, especially painting and sculpture, where religious iconography should be directed to sacramental mystagogy. A solid knowledge of the history of sacred art can be advantageous for those responsible for commissioning artists and architects to create works of art for the liturgy. Consequently it is essential that the education of seminarians and priests include the study of art history, with special reference to sacred buildings and the corresponding liturgical norms. Everything related to the Eucharist should be marked by beauty. Special respect and care must also be given to the vestments, the furnishings and the sacred vessels, so that by their harmonious and orderly arrangement they will foster awe for the mystery of God, manifest the unity of the faith and strengthen devotion.[125]

Liturgical song

42. In the *ars celebrandi*, liturgical song has a pre-eminent place.[126] Saint Augustine rightly says in a famous sermon that "the new man sings a new song. Singing is an expression of joy and, if we consider the matter, an expression of love."[127] The People of God assembled for the liturgy sings the praises of God. In the course of her two-thousand-year history, the Church has created, and still creates, music and songs which represent a rich patrimony of faith and love. This heritage must not be lost. Certainly as far as the liturgy is concerned, we cannot say that one song is as good as another. Generic improvisation or the introduction of musical genres which fail to respect the meaning of the liturgy should be avoided. As an element of the liturgy, song should be well integrated into the overall celebration.[128] Consequently everything—texts, music, execution—ought to correspond to the meaning of the mystery being celebrated, the structure of the rite and

the liturgical seasons.[129] Finally, while respecting various styles and different and highly praiseworthy traditions, I desire, in accordance with the request advanced by the Synod Fathers, that Gregorian chant be suitably esteemed and employed[130] as the chant proper to the Roman liturgy.[131]

THE STRUCTURE
OF THE EUCHARISTIC CELEBRATION

43. After mentioning the more significant elements of the *ars celebrandi* that emerged during the Synod, I would now like to turn to some specific aspects of the structure of the eucharistic celebration which require special attention at the present time, if we are to remain faithful to the underlying intention of the liturgical renewal called for by the Second Vatican Council, in continuity with the great ecclesial tradition.

The intrinsic unity of the liturgical action
44. First of all, there is a need to reflect on the inherent unity of the rite of Mass. Both in catechesis and in the actual manner of celebration, one must avoid giving the impression that the two parts of the rite are merely juxtaposed. The liturgy of the word and the Eucharistic liturgy, with the rites of introduction and conclusion, "are so closely interconnected that they form but one single act of worship."[132] There is an intrinsic bond between the word of God and the Eucharist. From listening to the word of God, faith is born or strengthened (cf. *Rom* 10:17); in the Eucharist the Word made flesh gives himself to us as our spiritual food.[133] Thus, "from the two tables of the word of God and the Body of Christ, the Church receives and gives to the faithful the bread of life."[134] Consequently it must constantly be kept in mind that the word of God, read and proclaimed by the Church in the liturgy, leads to the Eucharist as to its own connatural end.

The liturgy of the word

45. Together with the Synod, I ask that the liturgy of the word always be carefully prepared and celebrated. Consequently I urge that every effort be made to ensure that the liturgical proclamation of the word of God is entrusted to well-prepared readers. Let us never forget that "when the Sacred Scriptures are read in the Church, God himself speaks to his people, and Christ, present in his own word, proclaims the Gospel."[135] When circumstances so suggest, a few brief words of introduction could be offered in order to focus the attention of the faithful. If it is to be properly understood, the word of God must be listened to and accepted in a spirit of communion with the Church and with a clear awareness of its unity with the sacrament of the Eucharist. Indeed, the word which we proclaim and accept is the Word made flesh (cf. *Jn* 1:14); it is inseparably linked to Christ's person and the sacramental mode of his continued presence in our midst. Christ does not speak in the past, but in the present, even as he is present in the liturgical action. In this sacramental context of Christian revelation,[136] knowledge and study of the word of God enable us better to appreciate, celebrate and live the Eucharist. Here too, we can see how true it is that "ignorance of Scripture is ignorance of Christ."[137]

To this end, the faithful should be helped to appreciate the riches of Sacred Scripture found in the lectionary through pastoral initiatives, liturgies of the word and reading in the context of prayer (*lectio divina*). Efforts should also be made to encourage those forms of prayer confirmed by tradition, such as the Liturgy of the Hours, especially Morning Prayer, Evening Prayer and Night Prayer, and vigil celebrations. By praying the Psalms, the Scripture readings and the readings drawn from the great tradition which are included in the Divine Office, we can come to a deeper experience of the Christ-event and the economy of salvation, which in turn can enrich our understanding and participation in the celebration of the Eucharist.[138]

The homily

46. Given the importance of the word of God, the quality of homilies needs to be improved. The homily is "part of the liturgical action,"[139]

and is meant to foster a deeper understanding of the word of God, so that it can bear fruit in the lives of the faithful. Hence ordained ministers must "prepare the homily carefully, based on an adequate knowledge of Sacred Scripture."[140] Generic and abstract homilies should be avoided. In particular, I ask these ministers to preach in such a way that the homily closely relates the proclamation of the word of God to the sacramental celebration[141] and the life of the community, so that the word of God truly becomes the Church's vital nourishment and support.[142] The catechetical and paraenetic aim of the homily should not be forgotten. During the course of the liturgical year it is appropriate to offer the faithful, prudently and on the basis of the three-year lectionary, "thematic" homilies treating the great themes of the Christian faith, on the basis of what has been authoritatively proposed by the Magisterium in the four "pillars" of the *Catechism of the Catholic Church* and the recent *Compendium*, namely: the profession of faith, the celebration of the Christian mystery, life in Christ and Christian prayer.[143]

The presentation of the gifts

47. The Synod Fathers also drew attention to the presentation of the gifts. This is not to be viewed simply as a kind of "interval" between the liturgy of the word and the liturgy of the Eucharist. To do so would tend to weaken, at the least, the sense of a single rite made up of two interrelated parts. This humble and simple gesture is actually very significant: in the bread and wine that we bring to the altar, all creation is taken up by Christ the Redeemer to be transformed and presented to the Father.[144] In this way we also bring to the altar all the pain and suffering of the world, in the certainty that everything has value in God's eyes. The authentic meaning of this gesture can be clearly expressed without the need for undue emphasis or complexity. It enables us to appreciate how God invites man to participate in bringing to fulfillment his handiwork, and in so doing, gives human labor its authentic meaning, since, through the celebration of the Eucharist, it is united to the redemptive sacrifice of Christ.

The Eucharistic Prayer

48. The Eucharistic Prayer is "the center and summit of the entire celebration."[145] Its importance deserves to be adequately emphasized. The different Eucharistic Prayers contained in the Missal have been handed down to us by the Church's living Tradition and are noteworthy for their inexhaustible theological and spiritual richness. The faithful need to be enabled to appreciate that richness. Here the *General Instruction of the Roman Missal* can help, with its list of the basic elements of every Eucharistic Prayer: thanksgiving, acclamation, epiclesis, institution narrative and consecration, anamnesis, offering, intercessions and final doxology.[146] In a particular way, eucharistic spirituality and theological reflection are enriched if we contemplate in the anaphora the profound unity between the invocation of the Holy Spirit and the institution narrative[147] whereby "the sacrifice is carried out which Christ himself instituted at the Last Supper."[148] Indeed, "the Church implores the power of the Holy Spirit that the gifts offered by human hands be consecrated, that is, become Christ's Body and Blood, and that the spotless Victim to be received in communion be for the salvation of those who will partake of it."[149]

The sign of peace

49. By its nature the Eucharist is the sacrament of peace. At Mass this dimension of the eucharistic mystery finds specific expression in the sign of peace. Certainly this sign has great value (cf. *Jn* 14:27). In our times, fraught with fear and conflict, this gesture has become particularly eloquent, as the Church has become increasingly conscious of her responsibility to pray insistently for the gift of peace and unity for herself and for the whole human family. Certainly there is an irrepressible desire for peace present in every heart. The Church gives voice to the hope for peace and reconciliation rising up from every man and woman of good will, directing it towards the one who "is our peace" (*Eph* 2:14) and who can bring peace to individuals and peoples when all human efforts fail. We can thus understand the emotion so often felt during the sign of peace at a liturgical celebration. Even so, during the Synod of Bishops there was discussion about the appropriateness

of greater restraint in this gesture, which can be exaggerated and cause a certain distraction in the assembly just before the reception of Communion. It should be kept in mind that nothing is lost when the sign of peace is marked by a sobriety which preserves the proper spirit of the celebration, as, for example, when it is restricted to one's immediate neighbors.[150]

The distribution and reception of the Eucharist

50. Another moment of the celebration needing to be mentioned is the distribution and reception of Holy Communion. I ask everyone, especially ordained ministers and those who, after adequate preparation and in cases of genuine need, are authorized to exercise the ministry of distributing the Eucharist, to make every effort to ensure that this simple act preserves its importance as a personal encounter with the Lord Jesus in the sacrament. For the rules governing correct practice in this regard, I would refer to those documents recently issued on the subject.[151] All Christian communities are to observe the current norms faithfully, seeing in them an expression of the faith and love with which we all must regard this sublime sacrament. Furthermore, the precious time of thanksgiving after communion should not be neglected: besides the singing of an appropriate hymn, it can also be most helpful to remain recollected in silence.[152]

In this regard, I would like to call attention to a pastoral problem frequently encountered nowadays. I am referring to the fact that on certain occasions—for example, wedding Masses, funerals and the like—in addition to practicing Catholics there may be others present who have long since ceased to attend Mass or are living in a situation which does not permit them to receive the sacraments. At other times members of other Christian confessions and even other religions may be present. Similar situations can occur in churches that are frequently visited, especially in tourist areas. In these cases, there is a need to find a brief and clear way to remind those present of the meaning of sacramental communion and the conditions required for its reception. Wherever circumstances make it impossible to ensure that the meaning of the Eucharist is duly appreciated, the appropriateness of replacing the celebration of the Mass with a celebration of the word of God should be considered.[153]

The dismissal: "Ite, missa est"

51. Finally, I would like to comment briefly on the observations of the Synod Fathers regarding the dismissal at the end of the eucharistic celebration. After the blessing, the deacon or the priest dismisses the people with the words: *Ite, missa est*. These words help us to grasp the relationship between the Mass just celebrated and the mission of Christians in the world. In antiquity, *missa* simply meant "dismissal." However in Christian usage it gradually took on a deeper meaning. The word "dismissal" has come to imply a "mission." These few words succinctly express the missionary nature of the Church. The People of God might be helped to understand more clearly this essential dimension of the Church's life, taking the dismissal as a starting-point. In this context, it might also be helpful to provide new texts, duly approved, for the prayer over the people and the final blessing, in order to make this connection clear.[154]

ACTUOSA PARTICIPATIO

Authentic participation

52. The Second Vatican Council rightly emphasized the active, full and fruitful participation of the entire People of God in the eucharistic celebration.[155] Certainly, the renewal carried out in these past decades has made considerable progress towards fulfilling the wishes of the Council Fathers. Yet we must not overlook the fact that some misunderstanding has occasionally arisen concerning the precise meaning of this participation. It should be made clear that the word "participation" docs not refer to mere external activity during the celebration. In fact, the active participation called for by the Council must be understood in more substantial terms, on the basis of a greater awareness of the mystery being celebrated and its relationship to daily life. The conciliar Constitution *Sacrosanctum Concilium* encouraged

the faithful to take part in the eucharistic liturgy not "as strangers or silent spectators," but as participants "in the sacred action, conscious of what they are doing, actively and devoutly."[156] This exhortation has lost none of its force. The Council went on to say that the faithful "should be instructed by God's word, and nourished at the table of the Lord's Body. They should give thanks to God. Offering the immaculate Victim, not only through the hands of the priest but also together with him, they should learn to make an offering of themselves. Through Christ, the Mediator, they should be drawn day by day into ever more perfect union with God and each other."[157]

Participation and the priestly ministry

53. The beauty and the harmony of the liturgy find eloquent expression in the order by which everyone is called to participate actively. This entails an acknowledgment of the distinct hierarchical roles involved in the celebration. It is helpful to recall that active participation is not per se equivalent to the exercise of a specific ministry. The active participation of the laity does not benefit from the confusion arising from an inability to distinguish, within the Church's communion, the different functions proper to each one.[158] There is a particular need for clarity with regard to the specific functions of the priest. He alone, and no other, as the tradition of the Church attests, presides over the entire eucharistic celebration, from the initial greeting to the final blessing. In virtue of his reception of Holy Orders, he represents Jesus Christ, the head of the Church, and, in a specific way, also the Church herself.[159] Every celebration of the Eucharist, in fact, is led by the Bishop, "either in person or through priests who are his helpers."[160] He is helped by a deacon, who has specific duties during the celebration: he prepares the altar, assists the priest, proclaims the Gospel, preaches the homily from time to time, reads the intentions of the Prayer of the Faithful, and distributes the Eucharist to the faithful.[161] Associated with these ministries linked to the sacrament of Holy Orders, there are also other ministries of liturgical service which can be carried out in a praiseworthy manner by religious and properly trained laity.[162]

The eucharistic celebration and inculturation

54. On the basis of these fundamental statements of the Second Vatican Council, the Synod Fathers frequently stressed the importance of the active participation of the faithful in the eucharistic sacrifice. In order to foster this participation, provision may be made for a number of adaptations appropriate to different contexts and cultures.[163] The fact that certain abuses have occurred does not detract from this clear principle, which must be upheld in accordance with the real needs of the Church as she lives and celebrates the one mystery of Christ in a variety of cultural situations. In the mystery of the Incarnation, the Lord Jesus, born of woman and fully human (cf. *Gal* 4:4), entered directly into a relationship not only with the expectations present within the Old Testament, but also with those of all peoples. He thus showed that God wishes to encounter us in our own concrete situation. A more effective participation of the faithful in the holy mysteries will thus benefit from the continued inculturation of the eucharistic celebration, with due regard for the possibilities for adaptation provided in the *General Instruction of the Roman Missal*,[164] interpreted in the light of the criteria laid down by the Fourth Instruction of the Congregation for Divine Worship and the Discipline of the Sacraments *Varietates Legitimae* of 25 January 1994[165] and the directives expressed by Pope John Paul II in the Post-Synodal Exhortations *Ecclesia in Africa*, *Ecclesia in America*, *Ecclesia in Asia*, *Ecclesia in Oceania* and *Ecclesia in Europa*.[166] To this end, I encourage Episcopal Conferences to strive to maintain a proper balance between the criteria and directives already issued and new adaptations,[167] always in accord with the Apostolic See.

Personal conditions for an "active participation"

55. In their consideration of the *actuosa participatio* of the faithful in the liturgy, the Synod Fathers also discussed the personal conditions required for fruitful participation on the part of individuals.[168] One of these is certainly the spirit of constant conversion which must mark the lives of all the faithful. Active participation in the eucharistic liturgy can hardly be expected if one approaches it superficially, without an examination of his or her life. This inner disposition can be fostered,

for example, by recollection and silence for at least a few moments before the beginning of the liturgy, by fasting and, when necessary, by sacramental confession. A heart reconciled to God makes genuine participation possible. The faithful need to be reminded that there can be no *actuosa participatio* in the sacred mysteries without an accompanying effort to participate actively in the life of the Church as a whole, including a missionary commitment to bring Christ's love into the life of society.

Clearly, full participation in the Eucharist takes place when the faithful approach the altar in person to receive communion.[169] Yet true as this is, care must be taken lest they conclude that the mere fact of their being present in church during the liturgy gives them a right or even an obligation to approach the table of the Eucharist. Even in cases where it is not possible to receive sacramental communion, participation at Mass remains necessary, important, meaningful and fruitful. In such circumstances it is beneficial to cultivate a desire for full union with Christ through the practice of spiritual communion, praised by Pope John Paul II[170] and recommended by saints who were masters of the spiritual life.[171]

Participation by Christians who are not Catholic

56. The subject of participation in the Eucharist inevitably raises the question of Christians belonging to Churches or Ecclesial Communities not in full communion with the Catholic Church. In this regard, it must be said that the intrinsic link between the Eucharist and the Church's unity inspires us to long for the day when we will be able to celebrate the Holy Eucharist together with all believers in Christ, and in this way to express visibly the fullness of unity that Christ willed for his disciples (cf. Jn 17:21). On the other hand, the respect we owe to the sacrament of Christ's Body and Blood prevents us from making it a mere "means" to be used indiscriminately in order to attain that unity.[172] The Eucharist in fact not only manifests our personal communion with Jesus Christ, but also implies full *communio* with the Church. This is the reason why, sadly albeit not without hope, we ask Christians who are not Catholic to understand and respect our conviction, which is grounded

in the Bible and Tradition. We hold that eucharistic communion and ecclesial communion are so linked as to make it generally impossible for non-Catholic Christians to receive the former without enjoying the latter. There would be even less sense in actually concelebrating with ministers of Churches or ecclesial communities not in full communion with the Catholic Church. Yet it remains true that, for the sake of their eternal salvation, individual non-Catholic Christians can be admitted to the Eucharist, the sacrament of Reconciliation and the Anointing of the Sick. But this is possible only in specific, exceptional situations and requires that certain precisely defined conditions be met.[173] These are clearly indicated in the *Catechism of the Catholic Church*[174] and in its *Compendium*.[175] Everyone is obliged to observe these norms faithfully.

Participation through the communications media

57. Thanks to the remarkable development of the communications media, the word "participation" has taken on a broader meaning in recent decades. We all gladly acknowledge that the media have also opened up new possibilities for the celebration of the Eucharist.[176] This requires a specific preparation and a keen sense of responsibility on the part of pastoral workers in the sector. When Mass is broadcast on television, it inevitably tends to set an example. Particular care should therefore be taken to ensure that, in addition to taking place in suitable and well-appointed locations, the celebration respects the liturgical norms in force.

Finally, with regard to the value of taking part in Mass via the communications media, those who hear or view these broadcasts should be aware that, under normal circumstances, they do not fulfill the obligation of attending Mass. Visual images can represent reality, but they do not actually reproduce it.[177] While it is most praiseworthy that the elderly and the sick participate in Sunday Mass through radio and television, the same cannot be said of those who think that such broadcasts dispense them from going to church and sharing in the eucharistic assembly in the living Church.

Active participation by the sick

58. In thinking of those who cannot attend places of worship for reasons of health or advanced age, I wish to call the attention of the whole Church community to the pastoral importance of providing spiritual assistance to the sick, both those living at home and those in hospital. Their situation was often mentioned during the Synod of Bishops. These brothers and sisters of ours should have the opportunity to receive sacramental communion frequently. In this way they can strengthen their relationship with Christ, crucified and risen, and feel fully involved in the Church's life and mission by the offering of their sufferings in union with our Lord's sacrifice. Particular attention needs to be given to the disabled. When their condition so permits, the Christian community should make it possible for them to attend the place of worship. Buildings should be designed to provide ready access to the disabled. Finally, whenever possible, eucharistic communion should be made available to the mentally handicapped, if they are baptized and confirmed: they receive the Eucharist in the faith also of the family or the community that accompanies them.[178]

Care for prisoners

59. The Church's spiritual tradition, basing itself on Christ's own words (cf. Mt 25:36), has designated the visiting of prisoners as one of the corporal works of mercy. Prisoners have a particular need to be visited personally by the Lord in the sacrament of the Eucharist. Experiencing the closeness of the ecclesial community, sharing in the Eucharist and receiving holy communion at this difficult and painful time can surely contribute to the quality of a prisoner's faith journey and to full social rehabilitation. Taking up the recommendation of the Synod, I ask Dioceses to do whatever is possible to ensure that sufficient pastoral resources are invested in the spiritual care of prisoners.[179]

Migrants and participation in the Eucharist

60. Turning now to those people who for various reasons are forced to leave their native countries, the Synod expressed particular gratitude to all those engaged in the pastoral care of migrants. Specific attention

needs to be paid to migrants belonging to the Eastern Catholic Churches; in addition to being far from home, they also encounter the difficulty of not being able to participate in the eucharistic liturgy in their own rite. For this reason, wherever possible, they should be served by priests of their rite. In all cases I would ask Bishops to welcome these brothers and sisters with the love of Christ. Contacts between the faithful of different rites can prove a source of mutual enrichment. In particular, I am thinking of the benefit that can come, especially for the clergy, from a knowledge of the different traditions.[180]

Large-scale concelebrations

61. The Synod considered the quality of participation in the case of large-scale celebrations held on special occasions and involving not only a great number of the lay faithful, but also many concelebrating priests.[181] On the one hand, it is easy to appreciate the importance of these moments, especially when the Bishop himself celebrates, surrounded by his presbyterate and by the deacons. On the other hand, it is not always easy in such cases to give clear expression to the unity of the presbyterate, especially during the Eucharistic Prayer and the distribution of Holy Communion. Efforts need to be made lest these large-scale concelebrations lose their proper focus. This can be done by proper coordination and by arranging the place of worship so that priests and lay faithful are truly able to participate fully. It should be kept in mind, however, that here we are speaking of exceptional concelebrations, limited to extraordinary situations.

The Latin language

62. None of the above observations should cast doubt upon the importance of such large-scale liturgies. I am thinking here particularly of celebrations at international gatherings, which nowadays are held with greater frequency. The most should be made of these occasions. In order to express more clearly the unity and universality of the Church, I wish to endorse the proposal made by the Synod of Bishops, in harmony with the directives of the Second Vatican Council,[182] that, with the exception of the readings, the homily and the prayer of

the faithful, such liturgies could be celebrated in Latin. Similarly, the better-known prayers[183] of the Church's tradition should be recited in Latin and, if possible, selections of Gregorian chant should be sung. Speaking more generally, I ask that future priests, from their time in the seminary, receive the preparation needed to understand and to celebrate Mass in Latin, and also to use Latin texts and execute Gregorian chant; nor should we forget that the faithful can be taught to recite the more common prayers in Latin, and also to sing parts of the liturgy to Gregorian chant.[184]

Eucharistic celebrations in small groups

63. A very different situation arises when, in the interest of more conscious, active and fruitful participation, pastoral circumstances favor small group celebrations. While acknowledging the formative value of this approach, it must be stated that such celebrations should always be consonant with the overall pastoral activity of the Diocese. These celebrations would actually lose their catechetical value if they were felt to be in competition with, or parallel to, the life of the particular Church. In this regard, the Synod set forth some necessary criteria: small groups must serve to unify the community, not to fragment it; the beneficial results ought to be clearly evident; these groups should encourage the fruitful participation of the entire assembly, and preserve as much as possible the unity of the liturgical life of individual families.[185]

INTERIOR PARTICIPATION IN THE CELEBRATION

Mystagogical catechesis

64. The Church's great liturgical tradition teaches us that fruitful participation in the liturgy requires that one be personally conformed to the mystery being celebrated, offering one's life to God in unity with the sacrifice of Christ for the salvation of the whole world. For this reason, the Synod of Bishops asked that the faithful be helped to make their interior dispositions correspond to their gestures and

words. Otherwise, however carefully planned and executed our liturgies may be, they would risk falling into a certain ritualism. Hence the need to provide an education in eucharistic faith capable of enabling the faithful to live personally what they celebrate. Given the vital importance of this personal and conscious *participatio*, what methods of formation are needed? The Synod Fathers unanimously indicated, in this regard, a mystagogical approach to catechesis, which would lead the faithful to understand more deeply the mysteries being celebrated.[186] In particular, given the close relationship between the *ars celebrandi* and an *actuosa participatio*, it must first be said that "the best catechesis on the Eucharist is the Eucharist itself, celebrated well."[187] By its nature, the liturgy can be pedagogically effective in helping the faithful to enter more deeply into the mystery being celebrated. That is why, in the Church's most ancient tradition, the process of Christian formation always had an experiential character. While not neglecting a systematic understanding of the content of the faith, it centered on a vital and convincing encounter with Christ, as proclaimed by authentic witnesses. It is first and foremost the witness who introduces others to the mysteries. Naturally, this initial encounter gains depth through catechesis and finds its source and summit in the celebration of the Eucharist. This basic structure of the Christian experience calls for a process of mystagogy which should always respect three elements:

a) It interprets the rites in the light of the events of our salvation, in accordance with the Church's living tradition. The celebration of the Eucharist, in its infinite richness, makes constant reference to salvation history. In Christ crucified and risen, we truly celebrate the one who has united all things in himself (cf. *Eph* 1:10). From the beginning, the Christian community has interpreted the events of Jesus' life, and the Paschal Mystery in particular, in relation to the entire history of the Old Testament.

b) A mystagogical catechesis must also be concerned with *presenting the meaning of the signs* contained in the rites. This is particularly important in a highly technological age like our own, which risks losing the ability to appreciate signs and symbols. More than simply conveying information, a mystagogical catechesis should be capable of making the faithful more sensitive to the language of signs and gestures which, together with the word, make up the rite.

c) Finally, a mystagogical catechesis must be concerned with bringing out the *significance of the rites for the Christian life* in all its dimensions—work and responsibility, thoughts and emotions, activity and repose. Part of the mystagogical process is to demonstrate how the mysteries celebrated in the rite are linked to the missionary responsibility of the faithful. The mature fruit of mystagogy is an awareness that one's life is being progressively transformed by the holy mysteries being celebrated. The aim of all Christian education, moreover, is to train the believer in an adult faith that can make him a "new creation," capable of bearing witness in his surroundings to the Christian hope that inspires him.

If we are to succeed in carrying out this work of education in our ecclesial communities, those responsible for formation must be adequately prepared. Indeed, the whole people of God should feel involved in this formation. Each Christian community is called to be a place where people can be taught about the mysteries celebrated in faith. In this regard, the Synod Fathers called for greater involvement by communities of consecrated life, movements and groups which, by their specific charisms, can give new impetus to Christian formation.[188] In our time, too, the Holy Spirit freely bestows his gifts to sustain the apostolic mission of the Church, which is charged with spreading the faith and bringing it to maturity.[189]

Reverence for the Eucharist

65. A convincing indication of the effectiveness of eucharistic catechesis is surely an increased sense of the mystery of God present among us. This can be expressed in concrete outward signs of reverence for the Eucharist which the process of mystagogy should inculcate in the faithful.[190] I am thinking in general of the importance of gestures and posture, such as kneeling during the central moments of the

Eucharistic Prayer. Amid the legitimate diversity of signs used in the context of different cultures, everyone should be able to experience and express the awareness that at each celebration we stand before the infinite majesty of God, who comes to us in the lowliness of the sacramental signs.

ADORATION AND EUCHARISTIC DEVOTION

The intrinsic relationship between celebration and adoration
66. One of the most moving moments of the Synod came when we gathered in Saint Peter's Basilica, together with a great number of the faithful, for eucharistic adoration. In this act of prayer, and not just in words, the assembly of Bishops wanted to point out the intrinsic relationship between eucharistic celebration and eucharistic adoration. A growing appreciation of this significant aspect of the Church's faith has been an important part of our experience in the years following the liturgical renewal desired by the Second Vatican Council. During the early phases of the reform, the inherent relationship between Mass and adoration of the Blessed Sacrament was not always perceived with sufficient clarity. For example, an objection that was widespread at the time argued that the eucharistic bread was given to us not to be looked at, but to be eaten. In the light of the Church's experience of prayer, however, this was seen to be a false dichotomy. As Saint Augustine put it: *"nemo autem illam carnem manducat, nisi prius adoraverit; peccemus non adorando*—no one eats that flesh without first adoring it; we should sin were we not to adore it."[191] In the Eucharist, the Son of God comes to meet us and desires to become one with us; eucharistic adoration is simply the natural consequence of the eucharistic celebration, which is itself the Church's supreme act of adoration.[192] Receiving the Eucharist means adoring him whom we receive. Only in this way do we become one with him, and are given, as it were, a foretaste of the beauty of the heavenly liturgy. The act of adoration outside Mass prolongs and intensifies all that takes place during the liturgical celebration itself. Indeed, "only in adoration can a profound and genuine reception

mature. And it is precisely this personal encounter with the Lord that then strengthens the social mission contained in the Eucharist, which seeks to break down not only the walls that separate the Lord and ourselves, but also and especially the walls that separate us from one another."[193]

The practice of eucharistic adoration

67. With the Synod Assembly, therefore, I heartily recommend to the Church's pastors and to the People of God the practice of eucharistic adoration, both individually and in community.[194] Great benefit would ensue from a suitable catechesis explaining the importance of this act of worship, which enables the faithful to experience the liturgical celebration more fully and more fruitfully. Wherever possible, it would be appropriate, especially in densely populated areas, to set aside specific churches or oratories for perpetual adoration. I also recommend that, in their catechetical training, and especially in their preparation for First Holy Communion, children be taught the meaning and the beauty of spending time with Jesus, and helped to cultivate a sense of awe before his presence in the Eucharist.

Here I would like to express appreciation and support for all those Institutes of Consecrated Life whose members dedicate a significant amount of time to eucharistic adoration. In this way they give us an example of lives shaped by the Lord's real presence. I would also like to encourage those associations of the faithful and confraternities specifically devoted to eucharistic adoration; they serve as a leaven of contemplation for the whole Church and a summons to individuals and communities to place Christ at the center of their lives.

Forms of eucharistic devotion

68. The personal relationship which the individual believer establishes with Jesus present in the Eucharist constantly points beyond itself to the whole communion of the Church and nourishes a fuller sense of membership in the Body of Christ. For this reason, besides encouraging individual believers to make time for personal prayer before the Sacrament of the Altar, I feel obliged to urge parishes and other church

groups to set aside times for collective adoration. Naturally, already existing forms of eucharistic piety retain their full value. I am thinking, for example, of processions with the Blessed Sacrament, especially the traditional procession on the Solemnity of *Corpus Christi*, the Forty Hours devotion, local, national and international Eucharistic Congresses, and other similar initiatives. If suitably updated and adapted to local circumstances, these forms of devotion are still worthy of being practiced today.[195]

The location of the tabernacle

69. In considering the importance of eucharistic reservation and adoration, and reverence for the sacrament of Christ's sacrifice, the Synod of Bishops also discussed the question of the proper placement of the tabernacle in our churches.[196] The correct positioning of the tabernacle contributes to the recognition of Christ's real presence in the Blessed Sacrament. Therefore, the place where the eucharistic species are reserved, marked by a sanctuary lamp, should be readily visible to everyone entering the church. It is therefore necessary to take into account the building's architecture: in churches which do not have a Blessed Sacrament chapel, and where the high altar with its tabernacle is still in place, it is appropriate to continue to use this structure for the reservation and adoration of the Eucharist, taking care not to place the celebrant's chair in front of it. In new churches, it is good to position the Blessed Sacrament chapel close to the sanctuary; where this is not possible, it is preferable to locate the tabernacle in the sanctuary, in a sufficiently elevated place, at the center of the apse area, or in another place where it will be equally conspicuous. Attention to these considerations will lend dignity to the tabernacle, which must always be cared for, also from an artistic standpoint. Obviously it is necessary to follow the provisions of the *General Instruction of the Roman Missal* in this regard.[197] In any event, final judgment on these matters belongs to the Diocesan Bishop.

PART III

The Eucharist, a Mystery
to Be Lived

"As the living Father sent me, and I live
because of the Father, so he who eats me
will live because of me" (Jn 6:57).

THE EUCHARISTIC FORM OF THE CHRISTIAN LIFE

Spiritual worship—logiké latreía (Rom 12:1)

70. The Lord Jesus, who became for us the food of truth and love,
speaks of the gift of his life and assures us that "if any one eats of this
bread, he will live for ever" (Jn 6:51). This "eternal life" begins in us
even now, thanks to the transformation effected in us by the gift of
the Eucharist: "He who eats me will live because of me" (Jn 6:57).
These words of Jesus make us realize how the mystery "believed" and
"celebrated" contains an innate power making it the principle of new
life within us and the form of our Christian existence. By receiving
the body and blood of Jesus Christ we become sharers in the divine
life in an ever more adult and conscious way. Here too, we can apply
Saint Augustine's words, in his *Confessions*, about the eternal *Logos*
as the food of our souls. Stressing the mysterious nature of this food,
Augustine imagines the Lord saying to him: "I am the food of grown
men; grow, and you shall feed upon me; nor shall you change me, like
the food of your flesh, into yourself, but you shall be changed into
me."[198] It is not the eucharistic food that is changed into us, but rather
we who are mysteriously transformed by it. Christ nourishes us by
uniting us to himself; "he draws us into himself."[199]

Here the eucharistic celebration appears in all its power as the
source and summit of the Church's life, since it expresses at once both
the origin and the fulfillment of the new and definitive worship of

God, the *logiké latreía*.[200] Saint Paul's exhortation to the Romans in this regard is a concise description of how the Eucharist makes our whole life a spiritual worship pleasing to God: "I appeal to you therefore, my brothers, by the mercies of God, to present your bodies as a living sacrifice, holy and acceptable to God, which is your spiritual worship" (*Rom* 12:1). In these words the new worship appears as a total self-offering made in communion with the whole Church. The Apostle's insistence on the offering of our bodies emphasizes the concrete human reality of a worship which is anything but disincarnate. The Bishop of Hippo goes on to say that "this is the sacrifice of Christians: that we, though many, are one body in Christ. The Church celebrates this mystery in the sacrament of the altar, as the faithful know, and there she shows them clearly that in what is offered, she herself is offered."[201] Catholic doctrine, in fact, affirms that the Eucharist, as the sacrifice of Christ, is also the sacrifice of the Church, and thus of all the faithful.[202] This insistence on sacrifice—a "making sacred"—expresses all the existential depth implied in the transformation of our human reality as taken up by Christ (cf. *Phil* 3:12).

The all-encompassing effect of eucharistic worship

71. Christianity's new worship includes and transfigures every aspect of life: "Whether you eat or drink, or whatever you do, do all to the glory of God" (*1 Cor* 10:31). Christians, in all their actions, are called to offer true worship to God. Here the intrinsically eucharistic nature of Christian life begins to take shape. The Eucharist, since it embraces the concrete, everyday existence of the believer, makes possible, day by day, the progressive transfiguration of all those called by grace to reflect the image of the Son of God (cf. *Rom* 8:29ff.). There is nothing authentically human—our thoughts and affections, our words and deeds—that does not find in the sacrament of the Eucharist the form it needs to be lived to the full. Here we can see the full human import of the radical newness brought by Christ in the Eucharist: the worship of God in our lives cannot be relegated to something private and individual, but tends by its nature to permeate every aspect of our existence. Worship pleasing to God thus becomes a new way of living

our whole life, each particular moment of which is lifted up, since it is lived as part of a relationship with Christ and as an offering to God. The glory of God is the living man (cf. *1 Cor* 10:31). And the life of man is the vision of God.[203]

Iuxta dominicam viventes—*living in accordance with the Lord's Day*
72. From the beginning Christians were clearly conscious of this radical newness which the Eucharist brings to human life. The faithful immediately perceived the profound influence of the eucharistic celebration on their manner of life. Saint Ignatius of Antioch expressed this truth when he called Christians "those who have attained a new hope," and described them as "those living in accordance with the Lord's Day" (*iuxta dominicam viventes*).[204] This phrase of the great Antiochene martyr highlights the connection between the reality of the Eucharist and everyday Christian life. The Christians' customary practice of gathering on the first day after the Sabbath to celebrate the resurrection of Christ—according to the account of Saint Justin Martyr[205]—is also what defines the form of a life renewed by an encounter with Christ. Saint Ignatius' phrase—"living in accordance with the Lord's Day"—also emphasizes that this holy day becomes paradigmatic for every other day of the week. Indeed, it is defined by something more than the simple suspension of one's ordinary activities, a sort of parenthesis in one's usual daily rhythm. Christians have always experienced this day as the first day of the week, since it commemorates the radical newness brought by Christ. Sunday is thus the day when Christians rediscover the eucharistic form which their lives are meant to have. "Living in accordance with the Lord's Day" means living in the awareness of the liberation brought by Christ and making our lives a constant self-offering to God, so that his victory may be fully revealed to all humanity through a profoundly renewed existence.

Living the Sunday obligation
73. Conscious of this new vital principle which the Eucharist imparts to the Christian, the Synod Fathers reaffirmed the importance of the Sunday obligation for all the faithful, viewing it as a wellspring

of authentic freedom enabling them to live each day in accordance with what they celebrated on "the Lord's Day." The life of faith is endangered when we lose the desire to share in the celebration of the Eucharist and its commemoration of the paschal victory. Participating in the Sunday liturgical assembly with all our brothers and sisters, with whom we form one body in Jesus Christ, is demanded by our Christian conscience and at the same time it forms that conscience. To lose a sense of Sunday as the Lord's Day, a day to be sanctified, is symptomatic of the loss of an authentic sense of Christian freedom, the freedom of the children of God.[206] Here some observations made by my venerable predecessor John Paul II in his Apostolic Letter *Dies Domini*[207] continue to have great value. Speaking of the various dimensions of the Christian celebration of Sunday, he said that it is *Dies Domini* with regard to the work of creation, *Dies Christi* as the day of the new creation and the Risen Lord's gift of the Holy Spirit, *Dies Ecclesiae* as the day on which the Christian community gathers for the celebration, and *Dies hominis* as the day of joy, rest and fraternal charity.

Sunday thus appears as the primordial holy day, when all believers, wherever they are found, can become heralds and guardians of the true meaning of time. It gives rise to the Christian meaning of life and a new way of experiencing time, relationships, work, life and death. On the Lord's Day, then, it is fitting that Church groups should organize, around Sunday Mass, the activities of the Christian community: social gatherings, programs for the faith formation of children, young people and adults, pilgrimages, charitable works, and different moments of prayer. For the sake of these important values—while recognizing that Saturday evening, beginning with First Vespers, is already a part of Sunday and a time when the Sunday obligation can be fulfilled—we need to remember that it is Sunday itself that is meant to be kept holy, lest it end up as a day "empty of God."[208]

The meaning of rest and of work

74. Finally, it is particularly urgent nowadays to remember that the day of the Lord is also a day of rest from work. It is greatly to be hoped that

this fact will also be recognized by civil society, so that individuals can be permitted to refrain from work without being penalized. Christians, not without reference to the meaning of the Sabbath in the Jewish tradition, have seen in the Lord's Day a day of rest from their daily exertions. This is highly significant, for *it relativizes work* and directs it to the person: work is for man and not man for work. It is easy to see how this actually protects men and women, emancipating them from a possible form of enslavement. As I have had occasion to say, "work is of fundamental importance to the fulfillment of the human being and to the development of society. Thus, it must always be organized and carried out with full respect for human dignity and must always serve the common good. At the same time, it is indispensable that people not allow themselves to be enslaved by work or to idolize it, claiming to find in it the ultimate and definitive meaning of life."[209] It is on the day consecrated to God that men and women come to understand the meaning of their lives and also of their work.[210]

Sunday assemblies in the absence of a priest

75. Rediscovering the significance of the Sunday celebration for the life of Christians naturally leads to a consideration of the problem of those Christian communities which lack priests and where, consequently, it is not possible to celebrate Mass on the Lord's Day. Here it should be stated that a wide variety of situations exists. The Synod recommended first that the faithful should go to one of the churches in their Diocese where the presence of a priest is assured, even when this demands a certain sacrifice.[211] Wherever great distances make it practically impossible to take part in the Sunday Eucharist, it is still important for Christian communities to gather together to praise the Lord and to commemorate the Day set apart for him. This needs, however, to be accompanied by an adequate instruction about the difference between Mass and Sunday assemblies in the absence of a priest. The Church's pastoral care must be expressed in the latter case by ensuring that the liturgy of the word—led by a deacon or a community leader to whom this ministry has been duly entrusted by competent authority—

is carried out according to a specific ritual prepared and approved for this purpose by the Bishops' Conferences.[212] I reiterate that only Ordinaries may grant the faculty of distributing holy communion in such liturgies, taking account of the need for a certain selectiveness. Furthermore, care should be taken that these assemblies do not create confusion about the central role of the priest and the sacraments in the life of the Church. The importance of the role given to the laity, who should rightly be thanked for their generosity in the service of their communities, must never obscure the indispensable ministry of priests for the life of the Church.[213] Hence care must be taken to ensure that such assemblies in the absence of a priest do not encourage ecclesiological visions incompatible with the truth of the Gospel and the Church's tradition. Rather, they should be privileged moments of prayer for God to send holy priests after his own heart. It is touching, in this regard, to read the words of Pope John Paul II in his *Letter to Priests* for Holy Thursday 1979 about those places where the faithful, deprived of a priest by a dictatorial regime, would meet in a church or shrine, place on the altar a stole which they still kept and recite the prayers of the eucharistic liturgy, halting in silence "at the moment that corresponds to the transubstantiation," as a sign of how "ardently they desire to hear the words that only the lips of a priest can efficaciously utter."[214] With this in mind, and considering the incomparable good which comes from the celebration of the Eucharist, I ask all priests to visit willingly and as often as possible the communities entrusted to their pastoral care, lest they remain too long without the sacrament of love.

A eucharistic form of Christian life, membership in the Church

76. The importance of Sunday as the *Dies Ecclesiae* brings us back to the intrinsic relationship between Jesus' victory over evil and death, and our membership in his ecclesial body. On the Lord's Day, each Christian rediscovers the communal dimension of his life as one who has been redeemed. Taking part in the liturgy and receiving the Body and Blood of Christ intensifies and deepens our belonging to the one who died for us (cf. *1 Cor* 6:19ff.; 7:23). Truly, whoever eats of

Christ lives for him. The eucharistic mystery helps us to understand the profound meaning of the *communio sanctorum*. Communion always and inseparably has both a vertical and a horizontal sense: it is communion with God and communion with our brothers and sisters. Both dimensions mysteriously converge in the gift of the Eucharist. "Wherever communion with God, which is communion with the Father, with the Son and with the Holy Spirit, is destroyed, the root and source of our communion with one another is destroyed. And wherever we do not live communion among ourselves, communion with the Triune God is not alive and true either."[215] Called to be members of Christ and thus members of one another (cf. *1 Cor* 12:27), we are a reality grounded ontologically in Baptism and nourished by the Eucharist, a reality that demands visible expression in the life of our communities.

The eucharistic form of Christian life is clearly an ecclesial and communitarian form. Through the Diocese and the parish, the fundamental structures of the Church in a particular territory, each individual believer can experience concretely what it means to be a member of Christ's Body. Associations, ecclesial movements and new communities—with their lively charisms bestowed by the Holy Spirit for the needs of our time—together with Institutes of Consecrated Life, have a particular responsibility for helping to make the faithful conscious that they *belong* to the Lord (cf. *Rom* 14:8). Secularization, with its inherent emphasis on individualism, has its most negative effects on individuals who are isolated and lack a sense of belonging. Christianity, from its very beginning, has meant fellowship, a network of relationships constantly strengthened by hearing God's word and sharing in the Eucharist, and enlivened by the Holy Spirit.

Spirituality and eucharistic culture

77. Significantly, the Synod Fathers stated that "the Christian faithful need a fuller understanding of the relationship between the Eucharist and their daily lives. Eucharistic spirituality is not just participation in Mass and devotion to the Blessed Sacrament. It embraces the whole of life."[216] This observation is particularly insightful, given our situation

today. It must be acknowledged that one of the most serious effects of the secularization just mentioned is that it has relegated the Christian faith to the margins of life as if it were irrelevant to everyday affairs. The futility of this way of living—"as if God did not exist"—is now evident to everyone. Today there is a need to rediscover that Jesus Christ is not just a private conviction or an abstract idea, but a real person, whose becoming part of human history is capable of renewing the life of every man and woman. Hence the Eucharist, as the source and summit of the Church's life and mission, must be translated into spirituality, into a life lived "according to the Spirit" (*Rom* 8:4ff.; cf. *Gal* 5:16, 25). It is significant that Saint Paul, in the passage of the *Letter to the Romans* where he invites his hearers to offer the new spiritual worship, also speaks of the need for a change in their way of living and thinking: "Do not be conformed to this world but be transformed by the renewal of your mind, that you may prove what is the will of God, what is good and acceptable and perfect" (12:2). In this way the Apostle of the Gentiles emphasizes the link between true spiritual worship and the need for a new way of understanding and living one's life. An integral part of the eucharistic form of the Christian life is a new way of thinking, "so that we may no longer be children tossed to and fro and carried about with every wind of doctrine" (*Eph* 4:14).

The Eucharist and the evangelization of cultures

78. From what has been said thus far, it is clear that the eucharistic mystery puts us *in dialogue* with various cultures, but also in some way *challenges* them.[217] The intercultural character of this new worship, this *logiké latreía*, needs to be recognized. The presence of Jesus Christ and the outpouring of the Holy Spirit are events capable of engaging every cultural reality and bringing to it the leaven of the Gospel. It follows that we must be committed to promoting the evangelization of cultures, conscious that Christ himself is the truth for every man and woman, and for all human history. The Eucharist becomes a criterion for our evaluation of everything that Christianity encounters

in different cultures. In this important process of discernment, we can appreciate the full meaning of Saint Paul's exhortation, in his *First Letter to the Thessalonians*, to "test everything; and hold fast to what is good" (5:21).

The Eucharist and the lay faithful

79. In Christ, Head of his Body, the Church, all Christians are "a chosen race, a royal priesthood, a holy nation, a people he claims for his own, to declare his wonderful deeds" (*1 Pet* 2:9). The Eucharist, as a mystery to be "lived," meets each of us as we are, and makes our concrete existence the place where we experience daily the radical newness of the Christian life. The eucharistic sacrifice nourishes and increases within us all that we have already received at Baptism, with its call to holiness,[218] and this must be clearly evident from the way individual Christians live their lives. Day by day we become "a worship pleasing to God" by living our lives as a vocation. Beginning with the liturgical assembly, the sacrament of the Eucharist itself commits us, in our daily lives, to doing everything for God's glory.

And because the world is "the field" (*Mt* 13:38) in which God plants his children as good seed, the Christian laity, by virtue of their Baptism and Confirmation, and strengthened by the Eucharist, are called to live out the radical newness brought by Christ wherever they find themselves.[219] They should cultivate a desire that the Eucharist have an ever deeper effect on their daily lives, making them convincing witnesses in the workplace and in society at large.[220] I encourage families in particular to draw inspiration and strength from this sacrament. The love between man and woman, openness to life, and the raising of children are privileged spheres in which the Eucharist can reveal its power to transform life and give it its full meaning.[221] The Church's pastors should unfailingly support, guide and encourage the lay faithful to live fully their vocation to holiness within this world which God so loved that he gave his Son to become its salvation (cf. *Jn* 3:16).

The Eucharist and priestly spirituality

80. The eucharistic form of the Christian life is seen in a very special way in the priesthood. Priestly spirituality is intrinsically eucharistic. The seeds of this spirituality are already found in the words spoken by the Bishop during the ordination liturgy: "Receive the oblation of the holy people to be offered to God. Understand what you do, imitate what you celebrate, and conform your life to the mystery of the Lord's Cross."[222] In order to give an ever greater eucharistic form to his existence, the priest, beginning with his years in the seminary, should make his spiritual life his highest priority.[223] He is called to seek God tirelessly, while remaining attuned to the concerns of his brothers and sisters. An intense spiritual life will enable him to enter more deeply into communion with the Lord and to let himself be possessed by God's love, bearing witness to that love at all times, even the darkest and most difficult. To this end I join the Synod Fathers in recommending "the daily celebration of Mass, even when the faithful are not present."[224] This recommendation is consistent with the objectively infinite value of every celebration of the Eucharist, and is motivated by the Mass's unique spiritual fruitfulness. If celebrated in a faith-filled and attentive way, Mass is formative in the deepest sense of the word, since it fosters the priest's configuration to Christ and strengthens him in his vocation.

The Eucharist and the consecrated life

81. The relationship of the Eucharist to the various ecclesial vocations is seen in a particularly vivid way in "the prophetic witness of consecrated men and women, who find in the celebration of the Eucharist and in eucharistic adoration the strength necessary for the radical following of Christ, obedient, poor and chaste."[225] Though they provide many services in the area of human formation and care for the poor, education and health care, consecrated men and women know that the principal purpose of their lives is "the contemplation of things divine and constant union with God in prayer."[226] The

essential contribution that the Church expects from consecrated persons is much more in the order of being than of doing. Here I wish to reaffirm the importance of the witness of virginity, precisely in relation to the mystery of the Eucharist. In addition to its connection to priestly celibacy, the eucharistic mystery also has an intrinsic relationship to consecrated virginity, inasmuch as the latter is an expression of the Church's exclusive devotion to Christ, whom she accepts as her Bridegroom with a radical and fruitful fidelity.[227] In the Eucharist, consecrated virginity finds inspiration and nourishment for its complete dedication to Christ. From the Eucharist, moreover, it draws encouragement and strength to be a sign, in our own times too, of God's gracious and fruitful love for humanity. Finally, by its specific witness, consecrated life becomes an objective sign and foreshadowing of the "wedding-feast of the Lamb" (*Rev* 19:7-9) which is the goal of all salvation history. In this sense, it points to that eschatological horizon against which the choices and life decisions of every man and woman should be situated.

The Eucharist and moral transformation

82. In discovering the beauty of the eucharistic form of the Christian life, we are also led to reflect on the moral energy it provides for sustaining the authentic freedom of the children of God. Here I wish to take up a discussion that took place during the Synod about the connection between the *eucharistic form of life* and *moral transformation*. Pope John Paul II stated that the moral life "has the value of a 'spiritual worship' (*Rom* 12:1; cf. *Phil* 3:3), flowing from and nourished by that inexhaustible source of holiness and glorification of God which is found in the sacraments, especially in the Eucharist: by sharing in the sacrifice of the Cross, the Christian partakes of Christ's self-giving love and is equipped and committed to live this same charity in all his thoughts and deeds."[228] In a word, "'worship' itself, eucharistic communion, includes the reality both of being loved and of loving others in turn. A Eucharist which does not pass over into the concrete practice of love is intrinsically fragmented."[229]

This appeal to the moral value of spiritual worship should not be interpreted in a merely moralistic way. It is before all else the joy-filled discovery of love at work in the hearts of those who accept the Lord's gift, abandon themselves to him and thus find true freedom. The moral transformation implicit in the new worship instituted by Christ is a heartfelt yearning to respond to the Lord's love with one's whole being, while remaining ever conscious of one's own weakness. This is clearly reflected in the Gospel story of Zacchaeus (cf. *Lk* 19:1-10). After welcoming Jesus to his home, the tax collector is completely changed: he decides to give half of his possessions to the poor and to repay fourfold those whom he had defrauded. The moral urgency born of welcoming Jesus into our lives is the fruit of gratitude for having experienced the Lord's unmerited closeness.

Eucharistic consistency

83. Here it is important to consider what the Synod Fathers described as *eucharistic consistency*, a quality which our lives are objectively called to embody. Worship pleasing to God can never be a purely private matter, without consequences for our relationships with others: it demands a public witness to our faith. Evidently, this is true for all the baptized, yet it is especially incumbent upon those who, by virtue of their social or political position, must make decisions regarding fundamental values, such as respect for human life, its defense from conception to natural death, the family built upon marriage between a man and a woman, the freedom to educate one's children and the promotion of the common good in all its forms.[230] These values are not negotiable. Consequently, Catholic politicians and legislators, conscious of their grave responsibility before society, must feel particularly bound, on the basis of a properly formed conscience, to introduce and support laws inspired by values grounded in human nature.[231] There is an objective connection here with the Eucharist (cf. *1 Cor* 11:27-29). Bishops are bound to reaffirm constantly these values as part of their responsibility to the flock entrusted to them.[232]

THE EUCHARIST, A MYSTERY TO BE PROCLAIMED

The Eucharist and mission

84. In my homily at the eucharistic celebration solemnly inaugurating my Petrine ministry, I said that "there is nothing more beautiful than to be surprised by the Gospel, by the encounter with Christ. There is nothing more beautiful than to know him and to speak to others of our friendship with him."[233] These words are all the more significant if we think of the mystery of the Eucharist. The love that we celebrate in the sacrament is not something we can keep to ourselves. By its very nature it demands to be shared with all. What the world needs is God's love; it needs to encounter Christ and to believe in him. The Eucharist is thus the source and summit not only of the Church's life, but also of her mission: "an authentically eucharistic Church is a missionary Church."[234] We too must be able to tell our brothers and sisters with conviction: "That which we have seen and heard we proclaim also to you, so that you may have fellowship with us" (*1 Jn* 1:3). Truly, nothing is more beautiful than to know Christ and to make him known to others. The institution of the Eucharist, for that matter, anticipates the very heart of Jesus' mission: he is the one sent by the Father for the redemption of the world (cf. *Jn* 3:16-17; *Rom* 8:32). At the Last Supper, Jesus entrusts to his disciples the sacrament which makes present his self-sacrifice for the salvation of us all, in obedience to the Father's will. We cannot approach the eucharistic table without being drawn into the mission which, beginning in the very heart of God, is meant to reach all people. Missionary outreach is thus an essential part of the eucharistic form of the Christian life.

The Eucharist and witness

85. The first and fundamental mission that we receive from the sacred mysteries we celebrate is that of bearing witness by our lives. The wonder we experience at the gift God has made to us in Christ gives new impulse to our lives and commits us to becoming witnesses of his love. We become witnesses when, through our actions, words and way of being, Another makes himself present. Witness could be described

as the means by which the truth of God's love comes to men and women in history, inviting them to accept freely this radical newness. Through witness, God lays himself open, one might say, to the risk of human freedom. Jesus himself is the faithful and true witness (cf. *Rev* 1:5; 3:14), the one who came to testify to the truth (cf. *Jn* 18:37). Here I would like to reflect on a notion dear to the early Christians, which also speaks eloquently to us today: namely, witness even to the offering of one's own life, to the point of martyrdom. Throughout the history of the Church, this has always been seen as the culmination of the new spiritual worship: "Offer your bodies" (*Rom* 12:1). One thinks, for example, of the account of the martyrdom of Saint Polycarp of Smyrna, a disciple of Saint John: the entire drama is described as a liturgy, with the martyr himself becoming Eucharist.[235] We might also recall the eucharistic imagery with which Saint Ignatius of Antioch describes his own imminent martyrdom: he sees himself as "God's wheat" and desires to become in martyrdom "Christ's pure bread."[236] The Christian who offers his life in martyrdom enters into full communion with the Pasch of Jesus Christ and thus becomes Eucharist with him. Today too, the Church does not lack martyrs who offer the supreme witness to God's love. Even if the test of martyrdom is not asked of us, we know that worship pleasing to God demands that we should be inwardly prepared for it.[237] Such worship culminates in the joyful and convincing testimony of a consistent Christian life, wherever the Lord calls us to be his witnesses.

Christ Jesus, the one Savior

86. Emphasis on the intrinsic relationship between the Eucharist and mission also leads to a rediscovery of the ultimate content of our proclamation. The more ardent the love for the Eucharist in the hearts of the Christian people, the more clearly will they recognize the goal of all mission: *to bring Christ to others*. Not just a theory or a way of life inspired by Christ, but the gift of his very person. Anyone who has not shared the truth of love with his brothers and sisters has not yet given enough. The Eucharist, as the sacrament of our salvation, inevitably reminds us of the unicity of Christ and the salvation that he

won for us by his blood. The mystery of the Eucharist, believed in and celebrated, demands a constant catechesis on the need for all to engage in a missionary effort centered on the proclamation of Jesus as the one Savior.[238] This will help to avoid a reductive and purely sociological understanding of the vital work of human promotion present in every authentic process of evangelization.

Freedom of worship

87. In this context, I wish to reiterate the concern expressed by the Synod Fathers about the grave difficulties affecting the mission of those Christian communities in areas where Christians are a minority or where they are denied religious freedom.[239] We should surely give thanks to the Lord for all those Bishops, priests, consecrated persons and laity who devote themselves generously to the preaching of the Gospel and practice their faith at the risk of their lives. In not a few parts of the world, simply going to church represents a heroic witness that can result in marginalization and violence. Here too, I would like to reaffirm the solidarity of the whole Church with those who are denied freedom of worship. As we know, wherever religious freedom is lacking, people lack the most meaningful freedom of all, since it is through faith that men and women express their deepest decision about the ultimate meaning of their lives. Let us pray, therefore, for greater religious freedom in every nation, so that Christians, as well as the followers of other religions, can freely express their convictions, both as individuals and as communities.

THE EUCHARIST, A MYSTERY TO BE OFFERED TO THE WORLD

The Eucharist, bread broken for the life of the world

88. "The bread I will give is my flesh, for the life of the world" (*Jn* 6:51). In these words the Lord reveals the true meaning of the gift of his life for all people. These words also reveal his deep compassion for every man and woman. The Gospels frequently speak of Jesus' feelings

towards others, especially the suffering and sinners (cf. *Mt* 20:34; *Mk* 6:34; *Lk* 19:41). Through a profoundly human sensibility he expresses God's saving will for all people—that they may have true life. Each celebration of the Eucharist makes sacramentally present the gift that the crucified Lord made of his life, for us and for the whole world. In the Eucharist Jesus also makes us witnesses of God's compassion towards all our brothers and sisters. The eucharistic mystery thus gives rise to a service of charity towards neighbor, which "consists in the very fact that, in God and with God, I love even the person whom I do not like or even know. This can only take place on the basis of an intimate encounter with God, an encounter which has become a communion of will, affecting even my feelings. Then I learn to look on this other person not simply with my eyes and my feelings, but from the perspective of Jesus Christ."[240] In all those I meet, I recognize brothers or sisters for whom the Lord gave his life, loving them "to the end" (*Jn* 13:1). Our communities, when they celebrate the Eucharist, must become ever more conscious that the sacrifice of Christ is for all, and that the Eucharist thus compels all who believe in him to become "bread that is broken" for others, and to work for the building of a more just and fraternal world. Keeping in mind the multiplication of the loaves and fishes, we need to realize that Christ continues today to exhort his disciples to become personally engaged: "You yourselves, give them something to eat" (*Mt* 14:16). Each of us is truly called, together with Jesus, to be bread broken for the life of the world.

The social implications of the eucharistic mystery

89. The union with Christ brought about by the Eucharist also brings a newness to our social relations: "this sacramental 'mysticism' is social in character." Indeed, "union with Christ is also union with all those to whom he gives himself. I cannot possess Christ just for myself; I can belong to him only in union with all those who have become, or who will become, his own."[241] The relationship between the eucharistic mystery and social commitment must be made explicit.

The Eucharist is the sacrament of communion between brothers and sisters who allow themselves to be reconciled in Christ, who made of Jews and pagans one people, tearing down the wall of hostility which divided them (cf. *Eph* 2:14). Only this constant impulse towards reconciliation enables us to partake worthily of the Body and Blood of Christ (cf. *Mt* 5:23-24).[242] In the memorial of his sacrifice, the Lord strengthens our fraternal communion and, in a particular way, urges those in conflict to hasten their reconciliation by opening themselves to dialogue and a commitment to justice. Certainly, the restoration of justice, reconciliation and forgiveness are the conditions for building true peace.[243] The recognition of this fact leads to a determination to transform unjust structures and to restore respect for the dignity of all men and women, created in God's image and likeness. Through the concrete fulfillment of this responsibility, the Eucharist becomes in life what it signifies in its celebration. As I have had occasion to say, it is not the proper task of the Church to engage in the political work of bringing about the most just society possible; nonetheless she cannot and must not remain on the sidelines in the struggle for justice. The Church "has to play her part through rational argument and she has to reawaken the spiritual energy without which justice, which always demands sacrifice, cannot prevail and prosper."[244]

In discussing the social responsibility of all Christians, the Synod Fathers noted that the sacrifice of Christ is a mystery of liberation that constantly and insistently challenges us. I therefore urge all the faithful to be true promoters of peace and justice: "All who partake of the Eucharist must commit themselves to peacemaking in our world scarred by violence and war, and today in particular, by terrorism, economic corruption and sexual exploitation."[245] All these problems give rise in turn to others no less troubling and disheartening. We know that there can be no superficial solutions to these issues. Precisely because of the mystery we celebrate, we must denounce situations contrary to human dignity, since Christ shed his blood for all, and at the same time affirm the inestimable value of each individual person.

The food of truth and human need

90. We cannot remain passive before certain processes of globalization which not infrequently increase the gap between the rich and the poor worldwide. We must denounce those who squander the earth's riches, provoking inequalities that cry out to heaven (cf. *Jas* 5:4). For example, it is impossible to remain silent before the "distressing images of huge camps throughout the world of displaced persons and refugees, who are living in makeshift conditions in order to escape a worse fate, yet are still in dire need. Are these human beings not our brothers and sisters? Do their children not come into the world with the same legitimate expectations of happiness as other children?"[246] The Lord Jesus, the bread of eternal life, spurs us to be mindful of the situations of extreme poverty in which a great part of humanity still lives: these are situations for which human beings bear a clear and disquieting responsibility. Indeed, "on the basis of available statistical data, it can be said that less than half of the huge sums spent worldwide on armaments would be more than sufficient to liberate the immense masses of the poor from destitution. This challenges humanity's conscience. To peoples living below the poverty line, more as a result of situations to do with international political, commercial and cultural relations than as a result of circumstances beyond anyone's control, our common commitment to truth can and must give new hope."[247]

The food of truth demands that we denounce inhumane situations in which people starve to death because of injustice and exploitation, and it gives us renewed strength and courage to work tirelessly in the service of the civilization of love. From the beginning, Christians were concerned to share their goods (cf. *Acts* 4:32) and to help the poor (cf. *Rom* 15:26). The alms collected in our liturgical assemblies are an eloquent reminder of this, and they are also necessary for meeting today's needs. The Church's charitable institutions, especially *Caritas*, carry out at various levels the important work of assisting the needy, especially the poorest. Inspired by the Eucharist, the sacrament of charity, they become a concrete expression of that charity; they are to be praised and encouraged for their commitment to solidarity in our world.

The Church's social teaching

91. The mystery of the Eucharist inspires and impels us to work courageously within our world to bring about that renewal of relationships which has its inexhaustible source in God's gift. The prayer which we repeat at every Mass: "Give us this day our daily bread," obliges us to do everything possible, in cooperation with international, state and private institutions, to end or at least reduce the scandal of hunger and malnutrition afflicting so many millions of people in our world, especially in developing countries. In a particular way, the Christian laity, formed at the school of the Eucharist, are called to assume their specific political and social responsibilities. To do so, they need to be adequately prepared through practical education in charity and justice. To this end, the Synod considered it necessary for Dioceses and Christian communities to teach and promote the Church's social doctrine.[248] In this precious legacy handed down from the earliest ecclesial tradition, we find elements of great wisdom that guide Christians in their involvement in today's burning social issues. This teaching, the fruit of the Church's whole history, is distinguished by realism and moderation; it can help to avoid misguided compromises or false utopias.

The sanctification of the world and the protection of creation

92. Finally, to develop a profound eucharistic spirituality that is also capable of significantly affecting the fabric of society, the Christian people, in giving thanks to God through the Eucharist, should be conscious that they do so in the name of all creation, aspiring to the sanctification of the world and working intensely to that end.[249] The Eucharist itself powerfully illuminates human history and the whole cosmos. In this sacramental perspective we learn, day by day, that every ecclesial event is a kind of sign by which God makes himself known and challenges us. The eucharistic form of life can thus help foster a real change in the way we approach history and the world. The liturgy itself teaches us this, when, during the presentation of the gifts, the priest raises to God a prayer of blessing and petition over the bread and wine, "fruit of the earth," "fruit of the vine" and "work

of human hands." With these words, the rite not only includes in our offering to God all human efforts and activity, but also leads us to see the world as God's creation, which brings forth everything we need for our sustenance. The world is not something indifferent, raw material to be utilized simply as we see fit. Rather, it is part of God's good plan, in which all of us are called to be sons and daughters in the one Son of God, Jesus Christ (cf. *Eph* 1:4-12). The justified concern about threats to the environment present in so many parts of the world is reinforced by Christian hope, which commits us to working responsibly for the protection of creation.[250] The relationship between the Eucharist and the cosmos helps us to see the unity of God's plan and to grasp the profound relationship between creation and the "new creation" inaugurated in the resurrection of Christ, the new Adam. Even now we take part in that new creation by virtue of our Baptism (cf. *Col* 2:12ff.). Our Christian life, nourished by the Eucharist, gives us a glimpse of that new world—new heavens and a new earth—where the new Jerusalem comes down from heaven, from God, "prepared as a bride adorned for her husband" (*Rev* 21:2).

The usefulness of a Eucharistic Compendium

93. At the conclusion of these reflections, in which I have taken up a number of themes raised at the Synod, I also wish to accept the proposal which the Synod Fathers advanced as a means of helping the Christian people to believe, celebrate and live ever more fully the mystery of the Eucharist. The competent offices of the Roman Curia will publish a *Compendium* which will assemble texts from the *Catechism of the Catholic Church*, prayers, explanations of the Eucharistic Prayers of the Roman Missal and other useful aids for a correct understanding, celebration and adoration of the Sacrament of the Altar.[251] It is my hope that this book will help make the memorial of the Passover of the Lord increasingly the source and summit of the Church's life and mission. This will encourage each member of the faithful to make his or her life a true act of spiritual worship.

CONCLUSION

94. Dear brothers and sisters, the Eucharist is at the root of every form of holiness, and each of us is called to the fullness of life in the Holy Spirit. How many saints have advanced along the way of perfection thanks to their eucharistic devotion! From Saint Ignatius of Antioch to Saint Augustine, from Saint Anthony Abbot to Saint Benedict, from Saint Francis of Assisi to Saint Thomas Aquinas, from Saint Clare of Assisi to Saint Catherine of Siena, from Saint Paschal Baylon to Saint Peter Julian Eymard, from Saint Alphonsus Liguori to Blessed Charles de Foucauld, from Saint John Mary Vianney to Saint Thérèse of Lisieux, from Saint Pius of Pietrelcina to Blessed Teresa of Calcutta, from Blessed Piergiorgio Frassati to Blessed Ivan Mertz, to name only a few, holiness has always found its center in the sacrament of the Eucharist.

This most holy mystery thus needs to be firmly believed, devoutly celebrated and intensely lived in the Church. Jesus' gift of himself in the sacrament which is the memorial of his passion tells us that the success of our lives is found in our participation in the trinitarian life offered to us truly and definitively in him. The celebration and worship of the Eucharist enable us to draw near to God's love and to persevere in that love until we are united with the Lord whom we love. The offering of our lives, our fellowship with the whole community of believers and our solidarity with all men and women are essential aspects of that *logiké latreía*, spiritual worship, holy and pleasing to God (cf. *Rom* 12:1), which transforms every aspect of our human existence, to the glory of God. I therefore ask all pastors to spare no effort in promoting an authentically eucharistic Christian spirituality. Priests, deacons and all those who carry out a eucharistic ministry should always be able to find in this service, exercised with care and constant preparation, the strength and inspiration needed for their personal and communal path of sanctification. I exhort the lay faithful, and families in particular, to find ever anew in the sacrament of Christ's love the energy needed to make their lives an authentic sign of the presence of the risen Lord. I ask all consecrated men and women to show by their eucharistic lives the splendor and the beauty of belonging totally to the Lord.

95. At the beginning of the fourth century, Christian worship was still forbidden by the imperial authorities. Some Christians in North Africa, who felt bound to celebrate the Lord's Day, defied the prohibition. They were martyred after declaring that it was not possible for them to live without the Eucharist, the food of the Lord: *sine dominico non possumus*.[252] May these martyrs of Abitinae, in union with all those saints and beati who made the Eucharist the center of their lives, intercede for us and teach us to be faithful to our encounter with the risen Christ. We too cannot live without partaking of the sacrament of our salvation; we too desire to be *iuxta dominicam viventes*, to reflect in our lives what we celebrate on the Lord's Day. That day is the day of our definitive deliverance. Is it surprising, then, that we should wish to live every day in that newness of life which Christ has brought us in the mystery of the Eucharist?

96. May Mary Most Holy, the Immaculate Virgin, ark of the new and eternal covenant, accompany us on our way to meet the Lord who comes. In her we find realized most perfectly the essence of the Church. The Church sees in Mary—"Woman of the Eucharist," as she was called by the Servant of God John Paul II[253]—her finest icon, and she contemplates Mary as a singular model of the eucharistic life. For this reason, the priest, standing in the presence of the *verum Corpus natum de Maria Virgine* on the altar and speaking in the name of the liturgical assembly, says in the words of the canon: "We honor Mary, the ever-virgin mother of Jesus Christ our Lord and God."[254] Her holy name is also invoked and venerated in the canons of the Eastern Christian traditions. The faithful, for their part, "commend to Mary, Mother of the Church, their lives and the work of their hands. Striving to have the same sentiments as Mary, they help the whole

community to become a living offering pleasing to the Father."[255] She is the *tota pulchra*, the all-beautiful, for in her the radiance of God's glory shines forth. The beauty of the heavenly liturgy, which must be reflected in our own assemblies, is faithfully mirrored in her. From Mary we must learn to become men and women of the Eucharist and of the Church, and thus to present ourselves, in the words of Saint Paul, "holy and blameless" before the Lord, even as he wished us to be from the beginning (cf. *Col* 1:22; *Eph* 1:4).[256]

97. Through the intercession of the Blessed Virgin Mary, may the Holy Spirit kindle within us the same ardor experienced by the disciples on the way to Emmaus (cf. *Lk* 24:13-35) and renew our "eucharistic wonder" through the splendor and beauty radiating from the liturgical rite, the efficacious sign of the infinite beauty of the holy mystery of God. Those disciples arose and returned in haste to Jerusalem in order to share their joy with their brothers and sisters in the faith. True joy is found in recognizing that the Lord is still with us, our faithful companion along the way. The Eucharist makes us discover that Christ, risen from the dead, is our contemporary in the mystery of the Church, his body. Of this mystery of love we have become witnesses. Let us encourage one another to walk joyfully, our hearts filled with wonder, towards our encounter with the Holy Eucharist, so that we may experience and proclaim to others the truth of the words with which Jesus took leave of his disciples: "Lo, I am with you always, until the end of the world" (*Mt* 28:20).

Given in Rome, at Saint Peter's, on 22 February, the Feast of the Chair of Peter, in the year 2007, the second of my Pontificate.

NOTES

1   Cf. Saint Thomas Aquinas, *Summa Theologiae* III, q. 73, a. 3.

2   Saint Augustine, *In Iohannis Evangelium Tractatus*, 26,5: PL 35, 1609.

3   Benedict XVI, Address to Participants in the Plenary Assembly of the Congregation for the Doctrine of the Faith (10 February 2006): AAS 98 (2006), 255.

4   Benedict XVI, Address to the Members of the Ordinary Council of the General Secretariat of the Synod of Bishops (1 June 2006): *L'Osservatore Romano*, 2 June 2006, p. 5.

5   Cf. *Propositio* 2.

6   I am referring here to the need for a hermeneutic of continuity also with regard to the correct interpretation of the liturgical development which followed the Second Vatican Council: cf. Benedict XVI, Address to the Roman Curia (22 December 2005): AAS 98 (2006), 44-45.

7   Cf. AAS 97 (2005), 337-352.

8   *The Year of the Eucharist: Suggestions and Proposals* (15 October 2004): *L'Osservatore Romano*, 15 October 2004, Supplement.

9   Cf. AAS 95 (2003), 433-475. Also, the Instruction of the Congregation for Divine Worship and the Discipline of the Sacraments *Redemptionis Sacramentum* (25 March 2004): AAS 96 (2004), 549-601, expressly desired by John Paul II.

10   To name only the more important documents: Ecumenical Council of Trent, *Doctrina et canones de ss. Missae sacrificio*, DS 1738-1759; Leo XIII, Encyclical Letter *Mirae Caritatis* (28 May 1902): ASS (1903), 115-136; Pius XII, Encyclical Letter *Mediator Dei* (20 November 1947): AAS 39 (1947), 521-595; Paul VI, Encyclical Letter *Mysterium Fidei* (3 September 1965): AAS 57 (1965), 753-774; John Paul II, Encyclical Letter *Ecclesia de Eucharistia* (17 April 2003): AAS 95 (2003), 433-475; Congregation for Divine Worship and the Discipline of the Sacraments, Instruction *Eucharisticum Mysterium* (25 May 1967): AAS 59 (1967), 539-573; Instruction *Liturgiam Authenticam* (28 March 2001): AAS 93 (2001), 685-726.

11   Cf. *Propositio* 1.

12   No. 14: AAS 98 (2006), 229.

13   *Catechism of the Catholic Church*, 1327.

14   *Propositio* 16.

15   Benedict XVI, Homily at the Mass of Installation in the Cathedral of Rome (7 May 2005): AAS 97 (2005), 752.

16   Cf. *Propositio* 4.

17   *De Trinitate*, VIII, 8, 12: CCL 50, 287.

18   Encyclical Letter *Deus Caritas Est* (25 December 2005), 12: AAS 98 (2006), 228.

19   Cf. *Propositio* 3.

20   Roman Breviary, *Hymn for the Office of Readings of the Solemnity of Corpus Christi*.

21   Benedict XVI, Encyclical Letter *Deus Caritas Est* (25 December 2005), 13: AAS 98 (2006), 228.

22   Benedict XVI, Homily at Marienfeld Esplanade (21 August 2005): AAS 97 (2005), 891-892.

23   Cf. *Propositio* 3.

24   Cf. Roman Missal, *Eucharistic Prayer IV.*

25   *Cat.* XXIII, 7: PG 33, 1114ff.

26   Cf. *De Sacerdotio*, VI, 4: PG 48, 681.

27   *Ibid.*, III, 4: PG 48, 642.

28   *Propositio* 22.

29   Cf. *Propositio* 42: "This eucharistic encounter takes place in the Holy Spirit, who transforms and sanctifies us. He re-awakens in the disciple the firm desire to proclaim boldly to others all that he has heard and experienced, to bring them to the same encounter with Christ. Thus the disciple, sent forth by the Church, becomes open to a mission without frontiers."

30   Cf. Second Vatican Ecumenical Council, Dogmatic Constitution on the Church *Lumen Gentium*, 3; for an example, see: Saint John Chrysostom, *Catechesis* 3, 13-19: SC 50, 174-177.

31   John Paul II, Encyclical Letter *Ecclesia de Eucharistia* (17 April 2003), 1: AAS 95 (2003), 433.

32   *Ibid.*, 21: AAS 95 (2003), 447.

33   Cf. John Paul II, Encyclical Letter *Redemptor Hominis* (4 March 1979), 20: AAS 71 (1979), 309-316; Apostolic Letter *Dominicae Cenae* (24 February 1980), 4: AAS 72 (1980), 119-121.

34   Cf. *Propositio* 5.

35   Cf. Saint Thomas Aquinas, *Summa Theologiae*, III, q. 80, a. 4.

36   No. 38: AAS 95 (2003), 458.

37   Second Vatican Ecumenical Council, Dogmatic Constitution on the Church *Lumen Gentium*, 23.

38   Congregation for the Doctrine of the Faith, Letter on Some Aspects of the Church Understood as Communion *Communionis Notio* (28 May 1992), 11: AAS 85 (1993), 844-845.

39   *Propositio* 5. "The term 'catholic' expresses the universality deriving from the unity that the Eucharist, celebrated in each Church, fosters and builds up. The particular Churches in the universal Church thus have, in the Eucharist, the duty to make visible their own unity and diversity. This bond of fraternal love allows the trinitarian communion to become apparent. The Councils and Synods express in history this fraternal aspect of the Church."

40   Cf. *ibid.*

41   Decree on the Ministry and Life of Priests *Presbyterorum Ordinis*, 5.

42   Cf. *Propositio* 14.

43   Dogmatic Constitution on the Church *Lumen Gentium*, 1.

44   *De Orat. Dom.*, 23: PL 4, 553.

45   Second Vatican Ecumenical Council, Dogmatic Constitution on the Church *Lumen Gentium*, 48, cf. *ibid.*, 9.

46   Cf. *Propositio* 13.

47   Cf. Second Vatican Ecumenical Council, Dogmatic Constitution on the Church *Lumen Gentium*, 7.

48   Cf. *ibid.*, 11; Second Vatican Ecumenical Council, Decree on the Church's Missionary Activity *Ad Gentes*, 9, 13.

49   Cf. John Paul II, Apostolic Letter *Dominicae Cenae* (24 February 1980), 7: AAS 72 (1980), 124-127; Second Vatican Ecumenical Council, Decree on the Ministry and Life of Priests *Presbyterorum Ordinis*, 5.

50   Cf. *Code of Canons of the Eastern Churches*, can. 710.

51   Cf. *Rite of the Christian Initiation of Adults*, General Introduction, 34-36.

52   Cf. *Rite of Baptism for Children*, Introduction, 18-19.

53   Cf. *Propositio* 15.

54   Cf. *Propositio* 7; John Paul II, Encyclical Letter *Ecclesia de Eucharistia* (17 April 2003), 36: AAS 95 (2003), 457-458.

55   Cf. John Paul II, Post-Synodal Apostolic Exhortation *Reconciliatio et Paenitentia* (2 December 1984), 18: AAS 77 (1985), 224-228.

56   Cf. *Catechism of the Catholic Church*, 1385.

57   For example, the *Confiteor*, or the words of the priest and people before receiving Communion: *"Lord, I am not worthy to receive you, but only say the word and I shall be healed."* Not insignificantly does the liturgy also prescribe certain very beautiful prayers for the priest, handed down by tradition, which speak of the need for forgiveness, as, for example, the one recited quietly before inviting the faithful to sacramental communion: *"By the mystery of your body and blood, free me from all my sins and from every evil. Keep me always faithful to your teachings and never let me be parted from you."*

58   Cf. Saint John Damascene, *Exposition of the Faith*, IV, 9: PG 94, 1124C; Saint Gregory Nazianzen, *Oratio* 39, 17: PG 36, 356A; Ecumenical Council of Trent, *Doctrina de sacramento paenitentiae*, Chapter 2: DS 1672.

59   Cf. Second Vatican Ecumenical Council, Dogmatic Constitution on the Church *Lumen Gentium*, 11; John Paul II, Post-Synodal Apostolic Exhortation *Reconciliatio et Paenitentia* (2 December 1984), 30: AAS 77 (1985), 256-257.

60   Cf. *Propositio* 7.

61   Cf. John Paul II, Motu Proprio *Misericordia Dei* (7 April 2002): AAS 94 (2002), 452-459.

62   Together with the Synod Fathers I wish to note that the non-sacramental penitential services mentioned in the ritual of the sacrament of Reconciliation can be helpful for increasing the spirit of conversion and of communion in Christian communities, thereby preparing hearts for the celebration of the sacrament: cf. *Propositio* 7.

63   Cf. *Code of Canon Law*, can. 508.

64   Paul VI, Apostolic Constitution *Indulgentiarum Doctrina* (1 January 1967), *Norms*, No. 1: AAS 59 (1967), 21.

65   *Ibid.*, 9: AAS 59 (1967), 18-19.

66   Cf. *Catechism of the Catholic Church*, 1499-1532.

67   *Ibid.*, 1524.

68   Cf. *Propositio* 44.

69   Cf. Synod of Bishops, Second General Assembly, Document on the Ministerial Priesthood *Ultimis Temporibus* (30 November 1971): AAS 63 (1971), 898-942.

70   Cf. John Paul II, Post-Synodal Apostolic Exhortation *Pastores Dabo Vobis* (25 March 1992), 42-69: AAS 84 (1992), 729-778.

71   Cf. Second Vatican Ecumenical Council, Dogmatic Constitution on the Church *Lumen Gentium*, 10; Congregation for the Doctrine of the Faith, Letter on Certain Questions Concerning the Minister of the Eucharist *Sacerdotium Ministeriale* (6 August 1983): AAS 75 (1983), 1001-1009.

72   *Catechism of the Catholic Church*, 1548.

73   *Ibid.*, 1552.

74   Cf. *In Iohannis Evangelium Tractatus*, 123, 5: PL 35, 1967.

75   Cf. *Propositio* 11.

76   Cf. Decree on the Ministry and Life of Priests *Presbyterorum Ordinis*, 16.

77   Cf. John XXIII, Encyclical Letter *Sacerdotii Nostri Primordia* (1 August 1959): AAS 51 (1959), 545-579; Paul VI, Encyclical Letter *Sacerdotalis Coelibatus* (24 June 1967): AAS 59 (1967), 657-697; John Paul II, Post-Synodal Apostolic Exhortation *Pastores Dabo Vobis* (25 March 1992), 29: AAS 84 (1992), 703-705; Benedict XVI, Address to the Roman Curia (22 December 2006): *L'Osservatore Romano*, 23 December 2006, p. 6.

78   Cf. *Propositio* 11.

79   Cf. Second Vatican Ecumenical Council, Decree on Priestly Formation *Optatam Totius*, 6; Code of Canon Law, can. 241 § 1 and can. 1029; Code of Canons of the Eastern Churches, can. 342 § 1 and can. 758; John Paul II, Post-Synodal Apostolic Exhortation *Pastores Dabo Vobis* (25 March 1992), 11, 34, 50: AAS 84 (1992), 673-675; 712-714; 746-748; Congregation for the Clergy, Directory for the Ministry and Life of Priests *Dives Ecclesiae* (31 March 1994), 58; Congregation for Catholic Education, Instruction Concerning the Criteria for the Discernment of Vocations with Regard to Persons with Homosexual Tendencies in View of Their Admission to the Seminary and to Holy Orders (4 November 2005): AAS 97 (2005), 1007-1013.

80   Cf. *Propositio* 12; John Paul II, Post-Synodal Apostolic Exhortation *Pastores Dabo Vobis* (25 March 1992), 41: AAS 84 (1992), 726-729.

81   Second Vatican Ecumenical Council, Dogmatic Constitution on the Church *Lumen Gentium*, 29.

82   Cf. *Propositio* 38.

83   Cf. John Paul II, Post-Synodal Apostolic Exhortation *Familiaris Consortio* (22 November 1981), 57: AAS 74 (1982), 149-150.

84   Apostolic Letter *Mulieris Dignitatem* (15 August 1988), 26: AAS 80 (1988), 1715-1716.

85   *Catechism of the Catholic Church*, 1617.

86   Cf. *Propositio* 8.

87   Cf. Second Vatican Ecumenical Council, Dogmatic Constitution on the Church *Lumen Gentium*, 11.

88   Cf. *Propositio* 8.

89   Cf. John Paul II, Apostolic Letter *Mulieris Dignitatem* (15 August 1988): AAS 80 (1988), 1653-1729; Congregation for the Doctrine of the Faith, *Letter to the Bishops of the Catholic Church on the Collaboration of Men and Women in the Church and in the World* (31 May 2004): AAS 96 (2004), 671-687.

90   Cf. *Propositio 9.*

91   Cf. *Catechism of the Catholic Church,* 1640.

92   Cf. John Paul II, Post-Synodal Apostolic Exhortation *Familiaris Consortio* (22 November 1981), 84: AAS 74 (1982), 184-186; Congregation for the Doctrine of the Faith, Letter to the Bishops of the Catholic Church Concerning the Reception of Holy Communion by Divorced and Remarried Members of the Faithful *Annus Internationalis Familiae* (14 September 1994): AAS 86 (1994), 974-979.

93   Cf. Pontifical Council for Legislative Texts, Instruction on the Norms to Be Observed at Ecclesiastical Tribunals in Matrimonial Proceedings *Dignitas Connubii* (25 January 2005), Vatican City, 2005.

94   Cf. *Propositio 40.*

95   Benedict XVI, Address to the Tribunal of the Roman Rota for the Inauguration of the Judicial Year (28 January 2006): AAS 98 (2006), 138.

96   Cf. *Propositio 40.*

97   Cf. *ibid.*

98   Cf. *ibid.*

99   Cf. Second Vatican Ecumenical Council, Dogmatic Constitution on the Church *Lumen Gentium,* 48.

100   Cf. *Propositio 3.*

101   Here I would recall the words filled with hope and consolation found in Eucharistic Prayer II: "*Remember our brothers and sisters who have gone to their rest in the hope of rising again. Bring them and all the departed into the light of your presence.*"

102   Cf. Benedict XVI, Homily (8 December 2005): AAS 98 (2006), 15-16.

103   Dogmatic Constitution on the Church *Lumen Gentium,* 58.

104   *Propositio 4.*

105   *Relatio post disceptationem,* 4: *L'Osservatore Romano,* 14 October 2005, p. 5.

106   Cf. *Serm.* 1, 7; 11, 10; 22, 7; 29, 76: *Sermones dominicales ad fidem codicum nunc denuo editi,* Grottaferrata, 1977, pp. 135, 209ff., 292ff.; 337; Benedict XVI, *Message to Ecclesial Movements and New Communities* (22 May 2006): AAS 98 (2006), 463.

107   Cf. Second Vatican Ecumenical Council, Pastoral Constitution on the Church in the Modern World *Gaudium et Spes,* 22.

108   Cf. Second Vatican Ecumenical Council, Dogmatic Constitution on Divine Revelation *Dei Verbum,* 2, 4.

109   *Propositio 33.*

110   *Sermo* 227, 1: PL 38, 1099.

111   *In Iohannis Evangelium Tractatus,* 21, 8: PL 35, 1568.

112   *Ibid.,* 28, 1: PL 35, 1622.

113   Cf. *Propositio 30.* Weekday Masses, which the faithful are encouraged to attend, find their proper form on the day of the Lord, the day of Christ's resurrection; *Propositio 43.*

114   Cf. *Propositio* 2.

115   Cf. *Propositio* 25.

116   Cf. *Propositio* 19. *Propositio* 25 states: "An authentic liturgical action expresses the sacredness of the eucharistic mystery. This should be evident from the words and actions of the priest who celebrates, as he intercedes to God the Father both with the faithful and on their behalf."

117   *General Instruction of the Roman Missal,* 22; Second Vatican Ecumenical Council, Constitution on the Sacred Liturgy *Sacrosanctum Concilium,* 41; cf. Congregation for Divine Worship and the Discipline of the Sacraments, Instruction *Redemptionis Sacramentum* (25 March 2004), 19-25: AAS 96 (2004), 555-557.

118   Cf. Second Vatican Ecumenical Council, Decree on the Pastoral Office of Bishops in the Church *Christus Dominus,* 14; Constitution on the Sacred Liturgy *Sacrosanctum Concilium,* 41.

119   *General Instruction of the Roman Missal,* 22.

120   Cf. *ibid.*

121   Cf. *Propositio* 25.

122   Cf. Second Vatican Ecumenical Council, Constitution on the Sacred Liturgy *Sacrosanctum Concilium,* 112-130.

123   Cf. *Propositio* 27.

124   Cf. *ibid.*

125   In these matters the provisions of the *General Instruction of the Roman Missal,* 319-351, are to be faithfully observed.

126   Cf. *General Instruction of the Roman Missal,* 39-41; Second Vatican Ecumenical Council, Constitution on the Sacred Liturgy *Sacrosanctum Concilium,* 112-118.

127   *Sermo* 34, 1: PL 38, 210.

128   Cf. *Propositio* 25: "Like every artistic expression, singing must be closely adapted to the liturgy and contribute effectively to its aim; in other words, it must express faith, prayer, wonder and love of Jesus present in the Eucharist."

129   Cf. *Propositio* 29.

130   Cf. *Propositio* 36.

131   Cf. Second Vatican Ecumenical Council, Constitution on the Sacred Liturgy *Sacrosanctum Concilium,* 116; *General Instruction of the Roman Missal,* 41.

132   *General Instruction of the Roman Missal,* 28; cf. Second Vatican Ecumenical Council, Constitution on the Sacred Liturgy *Sacrosanctum Concilium,* 56; Sacred Congregation of Rites, Instruction *Eucharisticum Mysterium* (25 May 1967), 3: AAS 57 (1967), 540-543.

133   Cf. *Propositio* 18.

134   *Ibid.*

135   *General Instruction of the Roman Missal,* 29.

136   Cf. John Paul II, Encyclical Letter *Fides et Ratio* (14 September 1998), 13: AAS 91 (1999), 15-16.

137   Saint Jerome, *Comm. in Is., Prol.:* PL 24, 17; cf. Second Vatican Ecumenical Council, Dogmatic Constitution on Divine Revelation *Dei Verbum,* 25.

138   Cf. *Propositio* 31.

139   *General Instruction of the Roman Missal*, 29; cf. Second Vatican Ecumenical Council, Constitution on the Sacred Liturgy *Sacrosanctum Concilium*, 7, 33, 52.

140   Cf. *Propositio* 19.

141   Second Vatican Ecumenical Council, Constitution on the Sacred Liturgy *Sacrosanctum Concilium*, 52.

142   Second Vatican Ecumenical Council, Dogmatic Constitution on Divine Revelation *Dei Verbum*, 21.

143   To this end the Synod has called for the preparation of pastoral aids based on the three-year lectionary, to help connect the proclamation of the readings with the doctrine of the faith; cf. *Propositio* 19.

144   Cf. *Propositio* 20.

145   *General Instruction of the Roman Missal*, 78.

146   Cf. *ibid.*, 78-79.

147   Cf. *Propositio* 22.

148   *General Instruction of the Roman Missal*, 79d.

149   *Ibid.*, 79c.

150   Taking into account ancient and venerable customs and the wishes expressed by the Synod Fathers, I have asked the competent curial offices to study the possibility of moving the sign of peace to another place, such as before the presentation of the gifts at the altar. To do so would also serve as a significant reminder of the Lord's insistence that we be reconciled with others before offering our gifts to God (cf. Mt 5:23 ff.); cf. *Propositio* 23.

151   Cf. Congregation for Divine Worship and the Discipline of the Sacraments, Instruction *Redemptionis Sacramentum* (25 March 2004), 80-96: AAS 96 (2004), 574-577.

152   Cf. *Propositio* 34.

153   Cf. *Propositio* 35.

154   Cf. *Propositio* 24.

155   Cf. Second Vatican Ecumenical Council, Constitution on the Sacred Liturgy *Sacrosanctum Concilium*, 14-20; 30ff.; 48ff.; Congregation for Divine Worship and the Discipline of the Sacraments, Instruction *Redemptionis Sacramentum* (25 March 2004), 36-42: AAS 96 (2004), 561-564.

156   No. 48.

157   *Ibid.*

158   Cf. Congregation for the Clergy, Instruction on Certain Questions Regarding the Collaboration of the Non-Ordained Faithful in the Ministry of Priests *Ecclesiae de Mysterio* (15 August 1997): AAS 89 (1997), 852-877.

159   Cf. *Propositio* 33.

160   *General Instruction of the Roman Missal*, 92.

161   Cf. *ibid.*, 94.

162   Cf. Second Vatican Ecumenical Council, Decree on the Apostolate of the Laity
       Apostolicam Actuositatem, 24; *General Instruction of the Roman Missal*, 95-111;
       Congregation for Divine Worship and the Discipline of the Sacraments, Instruction
       Redemptionis Sacramentum (25 March 2004), 43-47: AAS 96 (2004), 564-566; *Propositio*
       33: "These ministries must be introduced in accordance with a specific mandate and
       in accordance with the real needs of the celebrating community. Those entrusted with
       these liturgical services must be chosen with care, well prepared, and provided with
       ongoing formation. Their appointment must be for a limited term. They must be known
       to the community and be gratefully acknowledged by the community."

163   Cf. Second Vatican Ecumenical Council, Constitution on the Sacred Liturgy *Sacrosanctum
       Concilium*, 37-42.

164   Cf. *General Instruction of the Roman Missal*, 386-399.

165   Cf. Congregation for Divine Worship and the Discipline of the Sacraments, Instruction
       on the Roman Liturgy and Inculturation *Varietates Legitimae* (25 January 1994): AAS 87
       (1995), 288-314.

166   Post-Synodal Apostolic Exhortation *Ecclesia in Africa* (14 September 1995), 55-71: AAS
       88 (1996), 34-47; Post-Synodal Apostolic Exhortation *Ecclesia in America* (22 January
       1999), 16, 40, 64, 70-72: AAS 91 (1999), 752-753, 775-776, 799, 805-809; Post-Synodal
       Apostolic Exhortation *Ecclesia in Asia* (6 November 1999), 21ff.: AAS 92 (2000), 482-
       487; Post-Synodal Apostolic Exhortation *Ecclesia in Oceania* (22 November 2001), 16:
       AAS 94 (2002), 382-384; Post-Synodal Apostolic Exhortation *Ecclesia in Europa* (28
       June 2003), 58-60: AAS 95 (2003), 685-686.

167   Cf. *Propositio* 26.

168   Cf. *Propositio* 35; Second Vatican Ecumenical Council, Constitution on the Sacred
       Liturgy *Sacrosanctum Concilium*, 11.

169   Cf. *Catechism of the Catholic Church*, 1388; Second Vatican Ecumenical Council,
       Constitution on the Sacred Liturgy *Sacrosanctum Concilium*, 55.

170   Cf. Encyclical Letter *Ecclesia de Eucharistia* (17 April 2003), 34: AAS 95 (2003), 456.

171   See, for example, Saint Thomas Aquinas, *Summa Theologiae*, III, q. LXXX, a. 1, 2; Saint
       Teresa of Jesus, *The Way of Perfection*, Chapter 35. The doctrine was authoritatively
       confirmed by the Council of Trent, Session XIII, c. VIII.

172   Cf. John Paul II, Encyclical Letter *Ut Unum Sint* (25 May 1995), 8: AAS 87 (1995), 925-
       926.

173   Cf. *Propositio* 41; Second Vatican Ecumenical Council, Decree on Ecumenism *Unitatis
       Redintegratio*, 8, 15; John Paul II, Encyclical Letter *Ut Unum Sint* (25 May 1995), 46:
       AAS 87 (1995), 948; Encyclical Letter *Ecclesia de Eucharistia* (17 April 2003), 45-46:
       AAS 95 (2003), 463-464; *Code of Canon Law*, can. 844 §§ 3-4; *Code of Canons of the
       Eastern Churches*, can. 671 §§ 3-4; Pontifical Council for Promoting Christian Unity,
       Directoire pour l'application des principes et des normes sur l'œcuménisme (25 March 1993),
       125, 129-131: AAS 85 (1993), 1087, 1088-1089.

174 Cf. Nos. 1398-1401.

175 Cf. No. 293.

176 Cf. Pontifical Council for Social Communications, Pastoral Instruction on Social Communications on the Twentieth Anniversary of "Communio et Progressio" *Aetatis Novae* (22 February 1992): AAS 84 (1992), 447-468.

177 Cf. *Propositio* 29.

178 Cf. *Propositio* 44.

179 Cf. *Propositio* 48.

180 Candidates for the priesthood can be introduced to these traditions as part of their seminary training: cf. *Propositio* 45.

181 Cf. *Propositio* 37.

182 Cf. Constitution on the Sacred Liturgy *Sacrosanctum Concilium*, 36, 54.

183 *Propositio* 36.

184 Cf. *ibid*.

185 Cf. *Propositio* 32.

186 Cf. *Propositio* 14.

187 *Propositio* 19.

188 Cf. *Propositio* 14.

189 Cf. Benedict XVI, Homily at First Vespers of Pentecost (3 June 2006): AAS 98 (2006), 509.

190 Cf. *Propositio* 34.

191 *Enarrationes in Psalmos* 98:9, CCL XXXIX, 1385; cf. Benedict XVI, Address to the Roman Curia (22 December 2005): AAS 98 (2006), 44-45.

192 Cf. *Propositio* 6.

193 Benedict XVI, Address to the Roman Curia (22 December 2005): AAS 98 (2006), 45.

194 Cf. *Propositio* 6; Congregation for Divine Worship and the Discipline of the Sacraments, *Directory on Popular Piety and the Liturgy* (17 December 2001), Nos. 164-165, Vatican City, 2002; Sacred Congregation of Rites, Instruction *Eucharisticum Mysterium* (25 May 1967): AAS 57 (1967), 539-573.

195 Cf. *Relatio post disceptationem*, 11: *L'Osservatore Romano*, 14 October 2005, p. 5.

196 Cf. *Propositio* 28.

197 Cf. No. 314.

198 VII, 10, 16: PL 32, 742.

199 Benedict XVI, Homily at Marienfeld Esplanade (21 August 2005): AAS 97 (2005), 892; cf. Homily for the Vigil of Pentecost (3 June 2006): AAS 98 (2006), 505.

200 Cf. *Relatio post disceptationem*, 6, 47: *L'Osservatore Romano*, 14 October 2005, pp. 5-6; *Propositio* 43.

201 *De Civitate Dei*, X, 6: PL 41, 284.

202 Cf. *Catechism of the Catholic Church*, 1368.

203 Cf. Saint Irenaeus, *Adv. Haer.*, IV, 20, 7: PG 7, 1037.

204 *Ad Magnes.*, 9, 1: PG 5, 670.

205 Cf. *I Apologia*, 67, 1-6; 66: PG 6, 430ff., 427, 430.

206 Cf. *Propositio* 30.

207 Cf. AAS 90 (1998), 713-766.

208 *Propositio* 30.

209 Homily (19 March 2006): AAS 98 (2006), 324.

210 The *Compendium of the Social Doctrine of the Church*, 258, rightly notes in this regard: "For man, bound as he is to the necessity of work, this rest opens to the prospect of a fuller freedom, that of the eternal Sabbath (cf. *Heb* 4:9-10). Rest gives men and women the possibility to remember and experience anew God's work, from Creation to Redemption, to recognize themselves as his work (cf. *Eph* 2:10), and to give thanks for their lives and for their subsistence to him who is their author."

211 Cf. *Propositio* 10.

212 Cf. *ibid.*

213 Cf. Benedict XVI, Address to the Bishops of Canada-Quebec During their Visit ad Limina (11 May 2006): cf. *L'Osservatore Romano*, 12 May 2006, p. 5.

214 No. 10: AAS 71 (1979), 414-415.

215 Benedict XVI, General Audience of 29 March 2006: *L'Osservatore Romano*, 30 March 2006, p. 4.

216 *Propositio* 39.

217 Cf. *Relatio post disceptationem*, 30: *L'Osservatore Romano*, 14 October 2005, p. 6.

218 Cf. Second Vatican Ecumenical Council, Dogmatic Constitution on the Church *Lumen Gentium*, 39-42.

219 Cf. John Paul II, Post-Synodal Apostolic Exhortation *Christifideles Laici* (30 December 1988), 14, 16: AAS 81 (1989), 409-413; 416-418.

220 Cf. *Propositio* 39.

221 Cf. *ibid.*

222 The *Roman Pontifical, Rites of Ordination of a Bishop, of Priests and of Deacons*, Ordination of a Priest, No. 163.

223 Cf. John Paul II, Post-Synodal Apostolic Exhortation *Pastores Dabo Vobis* (25 March 1992), 19-33; 70-81: AAS 84 (1992), 686-712; 778-800.

224 *Propositio* 38.

225 *Propositio* 39. Cf. John Paul II, Post-Synodal Apostolic Exhortation *Vita Consecrata* (25 March 1996), 95: AAS 88 (1996), 470-471.

226 *Code of Canon Law*, can. 663 § 1.

227 Cf. John Paul II, Post-Synodal Apostolic Exhortation *Vita Consecrata* (25 March 1996), 34: AAS 88 (1996), 407-408.

228 Encyclical Letter *Veritatis Splendor* (6 August 1993), 107: AAS 85 (1993), 1216-1217.

229 Benedict XVI, Encyclical Letter *Deus Caritas Est* (25 December 2005), 14: AAS 98 (2006), 229.

230 Cf. John Paul II, Encyclical Letter *Evangelium Vitae* (25 March 1995): AAS 87 (1995), 401-522; Benedict XVI, Address to the Pontifical Academy for Life (27 February 2006): AAS 98 (2006), 264-265.

231 Cf. Congregation for the Doctrine of the Faith, Doctrinal Note on Some Questions Regarding the Participation of Catholics in Political Life (24 November 2002): AAS 96 (2004), 359-370.

232 Cf. *Propositio* 46.

233 AAS 97 (2005), 711.

234 *Propositio* 42.

235 Cf. *Mart. Polycarp.*, XV, 1: PG 5, 1039, 1042.

236 Saint Ignatius of Antioch, *Ad. Rom.*, IV, 1: PG 5, 690.

237 Cf. Second Vatican Ecumenical Council, Dogmatic Constitution on the Church *Lumen Gentium*, 42.

238 Cf. *Propositio* 42; Congregation for the Doctrine of the Faith, Declaration on the Unicity and Salvific Universality of Jesus Christ and the Church *Dominus Iesus* (6 August 2000), 13-15: AAS 92 (2000), 754-755.

239 Cf. *Propositio* 42.

240 Benedict XVI, Encyclical Letter *Deus Caritas Est* (25 December 2005), 18: AAS 98 (2006), 232.

241 *Ibid.*, 14.

242 During the Synod sessions we heard very moving and significant testimonies about the effectiveness of the Eucharist in peacemaking. In this regard, *Propositio* 49 states that: "Thanks to eucharistic celebrations, peoples engaged in conflict have been able to gather around the word of God, hear his prophetic message of reconciliation through gratuitous forgiveness, and receive the grace of conversion which allows them to share in the same bread and cup."

243 Cf. *Propositio* 48.

244 Benedict XVI, Encyclical Letter *Deus Caritas Est* (25 December 2005), 28: AAS 98 (2006), 239.

245 *Propositio* 48.

246 Benedict XVI, Address to the Diplomatic Corps Accredited to the Holy See (9 January 2006): AAS 98 (2006), 127.

247 *Ibid.*

248 Cf. *Propositio* 48. In this regard, the *Compendium of the Social Doctrine of the Church* has proved most helpful.

249 Cf. *Propositio* 43.

250 Cf. *Propositio* 47.

251 Cf. *Propositio* 17.

252 *Martyrium Saturnini, Dativi et aliorum plurimorum*, 7, 9, 10: PL 8, 707, 709-710.

253 Cf. John Paul II, Encyclical Letter *Ecclesia de Eucharistia* (17 April 2003), 53: AAS 95 (2003), 469.

254 *Eucharistic Prayer I (Roman Canon)*.

255 *Propositio* 50.

256 Cf. Benedict XVI, Homily (8 December 2005): AAS 98 (2006), 15.